KinoSputnik

SHADOWS OF FORGOTTEN ANCESTORS

KinoSputnik

SHADOWS OF FORGOTTEN ANCESTORS

Sergei Paradjanov

Joshua First

intellect Bristol, UK / Chicago, USA

First published in the UK in 2016 by
Intellect, The Mill, Parnall Road, Fishponds, Bristol, BS16 3JG, UK

First published in the USA in 2016 by
Intellect, The University of Chicago Press, 1427 E. 60th Street,
Chicago, IL 60637, USA

A catalogue record for this book is available from the British Library.

Copy-editor: Michael Eckhardt
Cover designer: Emily Dann
Production manager: Matthew Floyd
Typesetting: Contentra Technologies

ISBN: 978-1-78320-709-1
ePDF: 978-1-78320-710-7
ePUB: 978-1-78320-711-4

KinoSputniks:
Series Editors: Birgit Beumers & Richard Taylor

Current titles:
Aleksandr Askoldov: The Commissar by Marat Grinberg
Sergei Paradjanov: Shadows of Forgotten Ancestors by Joshua First
Aleksandr Sokurov: Russian Ark by Birgit Beumers

CONTENTS

Note on transliteration

In this text, which contains both Russian and Ukrainian names and places, I use the Library of Congress system for transliterating from the Cyrillic to the Latin alphabet. I have departed from this system when a name has an accepted English spelling (e.g. Paradjanov instead of Paradzhanov; Tarkovsky instead of Tarkovskii; Eisenstein instead of Eizenshtein).

During the Soviet era, Ukrainian names were usually transliterated into English in their Russian variant; the film studied in this volume, however, was made in Ukrainian and therefore the names have been rendered using the Library of Congress system for Ukrainian. Place names, however, are given in the form that corresponds to the language of publication (in the bibliography) or their common English variant at the time (Kiev for Kyiv; L'vov for L'viv, etc.).

Acknowledgements

First and foremost, I am extremely grateful to Richard Taylor and Birgit Beumers for offering me the opportunity to write a book in the Kino Sputnik series, and for all of their help and patience along the way. Moreover, their scholarship, along with that of Denise Youngblood and Josephine Woll, inspired me to pursue the study of Soviet cinema almost twenty years ago. Most recently, James Steffen has helped me out tremendously with the present project, and his scholarship on Sergei Paradjanov continues to inspire my own work.

I owe an enormous debt of thanks to the many institutions and individuals who facilitated my research and writing. At the University of Michigan, the Center for Russian and East European Studies funded my study of the Ukrainian language, in addition to my first research trip to Kyiv in 2004. The Departments of History and Screen Arts and Cultures, in addition to the Rackham School of Graduate Studies, aided me immeasurably at key moments in my archival research. I conducted the bulk of my research in Kyiv and Moscow on an IREX fellowship in 2005–06. At the University of Mississippi, I received a summer research grant in 2015 that allowed me to complete the manuscript.

In Kyiv, I would like to thank the staff at the Central State Archive Museum of Literature and Art of Ukraine for going above and beyond their call of duty in getting essential research materials to me. I am grateful to have met Svetlana and Miron Petrovskii, who not only shared their flat during part of my research, but also for their personal recollections about *Shadows of Forgotten Ancestors* during its premiere on 4 September 1965.

While such support and inspiration was essential for completing this project, all views expressed in it, including faulty ones, are entirely my own.

KinoSputniks general editors' preface

This series intends to examine closely some key films to have emerged from the history of Russian and Soviet cinema. Continuing from *KinoFiles* (2000–2010), the *KinoSputniks* are intended for film enthusiasts and students alike, combining scholarship with a style of writing that is accessible to a broad readership. Each *KinoSputnik* is written by a specialist in the field of Russian and/or film studies, and examines the production, context and reception of the film, whilst defining the film's place in its national context and in the history of world cinema.

Birgit Beumers & Richard Taylor
Wales, June 2016

List of illustrations

Production credits

Production company:	Dovzhenko Film Studios, 1964
Release date:	4 September 1965 (premiere in Kiev)
Director:	Sergei Paradjanov
Screenplay:	Sergei Paradjanov and Ivan Chendei, based on Mykhailo Kotsiubyns'kyi's novella 'Tini zabutykh predkiv'/'Shadows of Forgotten Ancestors'
Assistant Directors:	Volodymyr Luhovs'kyi and Volodymyr Davydov
Cinematographer:	Iurii Illienko
Production Design:	Heorhii Iakutovych and Mykhailo Rakovs'kyi
Composer:	Myroslav Skoryk
Editor:	Maria Ponomarenko
Costume Design:	Lidiia Baikova
Screenplay Editor:	Oleksandr Syzonenko
Artistic Consultant:	Fedir Manailo
Running time:	92 minutes

CAST

Ivanko	Ivan Mykolaichuk; Ihor Dziura (child)
Marichka	Larisa Kadochnikova; Valentyna Hlyn'ko (child)
Palahna	Tat'iana Bestaeva
Iura the sorcerer	Spartak Bagashvili
Head shepherd	Mykola Hryn'ko
Myko	Leonid Engibarov
Ivanko's mother	Nina Alisova
Ivanko's father (Petro)	Oleksandr Hai
Marichka's father (Onufrii)	Oleksandr Raidanov
Marichka's mother (Paraska)	Neonila Hnepovs'ka

SCREENINGS AT INTERNATIONAL FILM FESTIVALS (AND AWARDS)

Mar del Plata (Argentina) International Film Festival, 1965 (Best Production)
San Sebastian International Film Festival, 1965
Venice International Film Festival, 1965
San Francisco International Film Festival, 1965
BFI London Film Festival, 1966
Thessaloniki International Film Festival, 1966 (Best Director)
New York International Film Festival, 1966
Melbourne International Film Festival, 1967

Plot summary

Set high in the Carpathian Mountains in the historic region of Bukovina, *Shadows of Forgotten Ancestors* tells the story of Ivanko, a Hutsul (one of several highland tribes in the Ukrainian-Romanian borderlands) boy who falls in love with Marichka, a girl from a rival family. The two children meet after the girl's father kills Ivanko's dad. They grow up together and secretly intend to marry. Marichka becomes pregnant, but has to spend the spring and summer alone as Ivanko tends sheep in a highland pasture. While separated, Marichka dies in an accident on the Cheremosh River. Receiving a supernatural premonition, Ivanko hurriedly descends to the village, only to find her body washed ashore. After a period of mourning, he marries Palahna, a young woman from a wealthy family. Although their wedding is an elaborate and joyous occasion, the two never love each other, and their marriage is one of convenience. Moreover, Palahna's unhappiness with Ivanko's inability (or unwillingness) to give her a child leads her to the arms of the village sorcerer. After witnessing their courtship in the village tavern, Ivanko threatens to kill the sorcerer, but ends up on the wrong side of an axe; as he dies, he has a vision of reuniting with Marichka in the forest. The film ends with a traditional Hutsul funeral for Ivanko, as the villagers alternately wail over his body, dance, smoke and cavort.

Chapter 1
Introduction

Unlike the majority of Soviet cinema's classic works, Sergei Paradjanov's *Tini zabutykh predkiv*/*Shadows of Forgotten Ancestors* is not a Russian film. Its language, setting, subject matter and methods of narration are distant from the established canon of the 1920s avant-garde, the classics of socialist realism, and the more recently acknowledged masterpieces of the Thaw. Moreover, Paradjanov made *Shadows* far from the centre of the Soviet film industry in Moscow, at the Aleksandr Dovzhenko Film Studios in Kiev (now Kyiv, Ukraine). Among its many accomplishments, *Shadows of Forgotten Ancestors* is often credited with founding the 'poetic school' in Soviet cinema, a loose grouping of films and film-makers interested in visual association, literary metaphor, folklore and non-Russian, generally ethnographic, topics. In the late 1960s and 1970s, 'poetic cinema' became shorthand for the best of 'national cinema'; that is to say, films made in the Soviet republics outside the Russian Soviet Federative Socialist Republic (RSFSR). In the Ukrainian Republic (Ukrainian SSR), *Shadows* heralded the birth of a Ukrainian dissident movement when its September 1965 premiere erupted in protest at recent arrests of Ukrainian intellectuals. The First Secretary of the Communist Party of Ukraine himself rejected 'poetic cinema' in 1974 as anti-Soviet, but the decade after *Shadows of Forgotten Ancestors* represented a veritable golden age for Ukrainian and other non-Russian cinema, and it was largely based on the influence of this one film.

Moreover, Paradjanov became a film-maker of global significance, largely owing to *Shadows*, even though he was and remains a mysterious figure. After graduating from Moscow's prestigious All-Union State Institute of Cinematography (Vsesoiuznyi gosudarstvennyi institut kinematografii, VGIK) in 1952, the Russian-speaking Armenian Paradjanov found work at the Ukrainian studio the following year. Forced to live in a Kiev dormitory for the next twelve years, Paradjanov worked on a number of mediocre projects at Dovzhenko Studios. During the production of *Shadows*, however, the director was catapulted to fame at the age of 40, both for his eccentric personal style and the film's ability to speak to contemporary concerns about Ukrainian folk culture. Despite the media frenzy that accompanied *Shadows* for a full year before it was released on the big screen in the USSR, and its success at international film festivals, the film did not enjoy wide release in the Soviet Union, and only about eleven million tickets were sold throughout the Soviet period. Moreover, the audience for the film during its initial run was only seven million, with most of the rest seeing it during perestroika (Ivanov 1973: 235).[2] Communist Party officials and authorities in film distribution (who had to fulfil their own financial plans) complained that audiences would not understand the film's complex imagery and opaque references to Ukrainian folklore.

In their standard textbook, *Film History: An Introduction*, Kristin Thompson and David Bordwell (2003: 460) call *Shadows of Forgotten Ancestors* 'a flurry of hysterically modernist techniques'. The line evokes the stylistically and generically eccentric nature of the film, which mixes static tableaux shots with a frantically mobile camera; a lyric love story situated securely in the Zeitgeist of the 1960s, but whose characters inhabit an isolated and ahistorical space of ancient myths and supernatural powers.

Apart from its 'poetic' techniques, what is it that made *Shadows* so exceptional for Soviet cinema that it continues to be celebrated with dozens of books and countless articles written in Ukrainian, Russian, Armenian, French and English? And what made the film so problematic for the authorities that it was eventually banned from screens in the country and contributed to its director's imprisonment (albeit almost a decade after its initial release)? The answer to both questions can be found in the ways in which *Shadows of Forgotten Ancestors* presents a bounded and distinct culture, one that could be appropriated as uniquely and authentically Ukrainian, rather than as generically Soviet or conflated with Russian. At the same time, Paradjanov and his cast (most notably, cinematographer Iurii Illienko) revealed a space, ripe with nationalistic value through a cosmopolitan, modernist lens, which was conversant with West European film movements such as Italian Neo-Realism and the French New Wave. Thus, the film was implicated not only as a text that might provoke 'bourgeois nationalism', but also as one overly concerned with the formalistic and apolitical aesthetics of art in the capitalist West. In this book, I examine such a strange film both on its own terms, and in the dual contexts of the Soviet Union during the 1960s and 1970s, along with the world of cinema during this exciting period. *Shadows of Forgotten Ancestors* is an interesting film for the simultaneously specific and global aesthetic and political spaces that it inhabited.

For these and other reasons, interest in Sergei Paradjanov's work has grown in recent years. Most notably, James Steffen's monograph *The Cinema of Sergei Parajanov* (2013) is a broad assessment of the director's filmography, methodically showing the development of his aesthetic sensibilities – from Ukraine in the 1950s and early 1960s, to Armenia in the late 1960s, and Georgia and Azerbaijan in the 1980s. Steffen (2013: 4) argues that Paradjanov's ethnographic interest in the non-Russian republics and 'old things' wed the avant-garde traditions of the Soviet 1920s to trends in contemporary European cinema, alongside a renewed interest in surrealism. My own study, *Ukrainian Cinema: Belonging and Identity during the Soviet Thaw* (First 2014), places Paradjanov's Ukrainian films within a broader cultural history of the 1960s more generally, and in Ukraine more specifically. In Ukraine, Paradjanov participated in, and created the conditions for, a contested national revival (First 2014). In a formal and theoretical analysis of *Shadows*, Robert Efird (2014) examines the distortion of perception and narrative alignment that lies at the heart of the film's unsettling aesthetic scheme. Moreover, several doctoral and MA theses have explored Sergei Paradjanov's contribution to world cinema (for example, see Gulyan 2013; Gurga 2012; Jakobsen 2014). The literature in Russian and Ukrainian on Paradjanov is extensive, ranging from serious scholarly analysis to memoir, and everything in between. Two figures, Kora Tsereteli and Larysa Briukhovets'ka, stand out for their dedication to studying the director and bringing his work to a wider audience in the former Soviet Union, even though they both continue to reproduce the myth of Sergei Paradjanov as a genius auteur.

To these ends, Chapter 2 explores the context and history of the film's production, which involved a difficult journey deep into the Carpathian Mountains in western Ukraine. The crew went far over budget to maintain the authenticity of the surroundings (which involved building a road to one of the locations) and the inclusion of 'real Hutsuls', the local inhabitants, as extras in the production, who supposedly improvised many of their lines and actions in the film. The stress of shooting in those conditions led to heated confrontations between members of the crew. These stories became the stuff of popular legend among the Kiev intelligentsia, including one where Paradjanov's cinematographer challenged him to a duel on the banks of the Cheremosh River using historic pistols common to Bukovina.[3]

Chapter 3 includes a sustained analysis of the film itself. First, I examine Paradjanov's ideas about the cinema. While Soviet authorities only allowed him to publish one article on film theory during his fraught career, he nonetheless laid out further principles in speeches, interviews and in conversations with others. How and to what degree did the director apply those theories to the making of *Shadows*? Second, this chapter explores connections between the film and other film movements at the beginning of the 1960s, both within the Soviet Union (such as 'poetic cinema') and in Western Europe. Finally, the chapter examines the film's claims to ethnographic authenticity, along with allusions to biblical, classical and Renaissance themes and visual art, and its relationship to socialist realism, the only officially sanctioned 'method' of artistic production.

The fourth and final chapter explores the reception and legacy of *Shadows of Forgotten Ancestors*. I examine the numerous controversies that followed *Shadows* from production to the screen. Paradjanov refused to allow a Russian dub of the film for general release, incurring the ire of the authorities. During its premiere in Kiev, Ukrainian dissidents disrupted the event by protesting the recent arrests of several Ukrainian intellectuals, which further pegged *Shadows* as a nationalist text. These controversies notwithstanding, the film received entirely favourable reviews in the Ukrainian and Russian press, made waves at film festivals around the world, and even saw a modest box-office return. After its initial run, *Shadows* returned to the screen for at least a few days every year until the end of the decade. The film was then shelved until perestroika, largely because of the influence it continued to have on other Soviet film-makers. In taking the story to the present, we find ever more insistent assertions of the significance of the film, especially in Ukraine, even as some critics and scholars complain of its unwieldy and overdetermined legacy for the nation (Briukhovets'ka 2012; Shevchuk 2005).

Chapter 2
Historical context and production history

The idea to make *Shadows of Forgotten Ancestors* came from a letter addressed to the director of Dovzhenko Studios in 1962. Iryna Kotsiubyns'ka asked that the studio adapt her father's 1912 novella of the same title in honour of the centenary of his birth (Korol' 2001: 319). Mykhailo Kotsiubyns'kyi's (1864–1913) original was an apolitical and Symbolist-inspired work, and might not have been the most likely choice for a Soviet film. Yet because of the Kotsiubyns'kyi family's importance in Ukraine, the studio accepted the assignment without much discussion, although they gave the project to an undistinguished but experienced director. Soviet culture thrived on anniversaries – be they Lenin's birthday, the anniversary of the October Revolution, the birth or death of a famous writer or artist, or the anniversary of a notable political tract, opera, novel, etc. The Dovzhenko Studios rarely had a year in which there were no anniversary films to make. Moreover, they were constantly fielding requests from the public to make such films, which, when released, were rarely successful at the box office. As 1964 drew near, film-makers in Kiev were significantly more preoccupied with the sesquicentennial of Ukraine's national poet, Taras Shevchenko (1814–61), than with the fairly minor Kotsiubyns'kyi event.

Iryna, the letter-writer, was the director of a small museum dedicated to her father's life and work in the provincial city of Chernigov (now Chernihiv), just north-east of Kiev. Her older brother, killed during the Stalinist Terror in 1937, had been an important Old Bolshevik and member of the Soviet Ukrainian government. Recently rehabilitated as part of Nikita Khrushchev's de-Stalinization, Iurii Kotsiubyns'kyi became the Ukrainian face within the Russian Revolution. Iryna and Iurii's father, Mykhailo, had vague left-wing leanings, and was friends with the writer and father of socialist realism, Maksim Gor'kii. In commemorating the Revolution, authorities and cultural producers had to grasp at straws to find its non-Russian agents. Consequently, Kotsiubyns'kyi the elder's revolutionary credentials were often exaggerated.

Many of his books, most notably *Shadows of Forgotten Ancestors*, were fixated on traditional folkways and the remnants of paganistic beliefs in the remote outposts of Ukrainian civilization in the East European borderlands. While certainly not an idyllic picture of the Ukrainian village, as social conflict was present in many of his works, the latter was not the point. After Stalin's death in 1953, a few of his short stories were adapted for the screen before Paradjanov's *Shadows*, most notably the acclaimed director Mark Donskoi's *Dorogoi tsenoi/At a High Price* (1957). This renewed interest in Kotsiubyns'kyi's work coincided with a critical repositioning of the writer's interest in a uniquely Ukrainian folklore and ethnography (Zinych 1964: 3). That said, however, the film's cinematographer, Iurii Illienko (2008b: 82), remembers that the Dovzhenko Studios' authorities presented the idea of *Shadows* to him as 'Socialist Realism about the class war among the Hutsuls', which would have been very difficult to tease out of Kotsiubyns'kyi.

When Paradjanov started working on the film in 1963, Ukraine's premiere film studio, Dovzhenko Studios, was peripheral to the broader currents in Soviet cinema during the Thaw. While some subsequently famous Soviet film-makers cut their teeth in Kiev and Odessa, they always left when Moscow called. Sergei Paradjanov's early work at the studio was typical of the studio during the late 1950s and early 1960s: he made a collective farm musical, *Pervyi paren'/The Top Guy* (1958); a World War II-themed melodrama called *Ukrainskaia rapsodiia/Ukrainian Rhapsody* (1961); and the anti-religious propaganda film *Tsvetok na kamne/Flower on the Stone* (1964). According to James Steffen (2013: 37–42, 45–55), Paradjanov's early films in Ukraine reveal an unusual combination of the film-maker's characteristic visual flair with the remnants of Stalin-era genre cinema. But because the former is only noteworthy in hindsight, such films did nothing to improve the Dovzhenko Studios' reputation, nor establish Paradjanov's. Despite his non-stellar career, Paradjanov had become quite the socialite in Kiev by the time he began his work on *Shadows*. Much of the city's intelligentsia knew him personally and considered him interesting, talented and highly intelligent, even though he could often be quite the windbag.

Paradjanov himself seemed embarrassed by these earlier films. His assistant director on *Shadows*, Volodymyr Luhovs'kyi (1998: 29), remembers that when the two of them passed a poster of *Flower on the Stone* at a cinema in downtown Kiev, Paradjanov 'waved his arm [and said,] "Oh… [that's] shit on a stone"'. He had taken the latter project after the first director was fired for complicity in the death of the leading actress, making it a challenging film to complete. Paradjanov's senior colleague Viktor Ivanov said during a 1962 studio meeting as everyone criticized him:

> I would give him a medal for bravery for *The Real Guy* [*Nastoiashchii paren'*, sic]. No one approached it at that time. No one wanted to make *Ukrainian Rhapsody* either. That was a difficult screenplay. He alone took on this project. You were the only person who came to the rescue on this picture [*Flower on the Stone*] and now it's easy for us to joke and complain.
>
> (TsDAMLMU 670/1/1536: 22)

Far from signifying a prestige project, Paradjanov's assignment to direct *Shadows of Forgotten Ancestors* implied that the studio just wanted someone to get it done.

Significant changes were under way at the Dovzhenko Studios in 1963, however, which ultimately transformed a project that was supposed to check off a box to one that occupied the entire studio's attention for more than two years. When authority for film production and distribution was transferred from the Ministry of Culture to a new State Committee for Cinematography (Goskino) in 1963, the journalist and film critic Sviatoslav Ivanov became the Ukrainian branch's (Derzhkino) first chairperson. Alongside this appointment, literary scholar Vasyl' Tsvirkunov replaced the unpopular and unqualified Volodymyr Nebera as the head of Dovzhenko Studios. Ivanov and Tsvirkunov were both professionals within literary and film criticism before serving in these positions, rather than merely watchdogs sent from the Central Committee of the Communist Party, and their commitment to improving Ukrainian cinema's reputation was evident from the beginning of their terms. They concentrated on attracting young talent from VGIK, which responded to a persistent critique of film-makers of the previous management. Paradjanov, for example, wrote a damning letter to industry and studio authorities in 1957, in which he condemned the studio for preventing young film-makers from working on independent projects, while continually favouring Muscovite directors or pre-war Ukrainian directors, most of whom were cribbed from the theatre. He claimed that the studio had lost all of its talented film-makers due to a 'lack of trust in people' (Paradzhanov 1990: 32–34). Ivanov and Tsvirkunov promised to trust young people at the studio, but they also insisted on the moral obligation of Ukrainians to stay in the Republic rather than leaving for the centre after a few years. They hoped to offer audiences both popular genre productions and prestige films, while remaining true to the studio's Ukrainian brand. Even though box-office returns for Ukrainian films actually dropped during the decade when they controlled the industry, Ivanov and Tsvirkunov were influential within the Central Committee of the Communist Party of Ukraine, and managed to impress upon the party boss, Petro Shelest, in particular, the need for sophisticated, literary-minded cinema. Without their influence and Shelest's blessing, Paradjanov's project would have remained marginal. As leaders who understood the director's potential, they gave Paradjanov an extraordinary amount of autonomy in its production. Moreover, his established reputation among the Kiev intelligentsia made *Shadows of Forgotten Ancestors* one of the most hyped films within the Ukrainian and, eventually, the Moscow press in 1964–65.

Paradjanov assembled a virtual 'who's who' of established and up-and-coming Ukrainian writers, artists and intellectuals to serve in the crew and as advisors. Among the older generation, Carpathian folklorist Ivan Chendei wrote the screenplay, Modernist painter Fedir Manailo served as artistic advisor, and novelist Oleksandr Syzonenko edited the screenplay. Paradjanov went to Moscow to personally select VGIK student Iurii Illienko as the cinematographer, who brought with him his fiancée, Larisa Kadochnikova, as the female lead in the film. He found the young graphic artist Heorhii Iakutovych to serve as the film's set designer after seeing his Hutsul and Carpathian themed lithographs and paintings exhibited in Kiev in the late 1950s and early 1960s (Briukhovets'ka 1999: 2). Ukraine's answer to Evgenii Evtushenko, Ivan Drach, served as a kind of unofficial literary advisor on the set. And the 25-year old composer Miroslav Skoryk from L'vov wrote the unusual score that mixed orchestral music with Carpathian folk melodies. Apart from Paradjanov himself, the entire crew was Ukrainian, and many of them were from the West Ukrainian regions of Galicia or Bukovina, both historically significant for Ukrainian culture and politically sensitive due to their more recent incorporation into the USSR.[4]

Despite Paradjanov's famous hospitality and eccentric graciousness, personal and professional conflicts plagued the production from the very beginning. Paradjanov was notoriously difficult to work with, often insulting his colleagues and even the studio authorities, albeit mostly in jest. He was convinced that he personally was making a fundamentally 'brilliant film' and that the studio should stop everything else it was doing to support *Shadows*, including giving him a 'million roubles' to complete the increasingly over-budget production (Luhovs'kyi 1998: 37–39, 79).[5] First, Paradjanov began taking apart Ivan Chendei's screenplay, supposedly with the help of the cast, crew and local Hutsuls, and would soon demand compensation and credit for these extensive edits. In the end, Chendei considered the director a traitor for his apparently greedy haggling over the honorarium.[6] Moreover, authorities at Goskino in Moscow had immediate reservations about the representation of religious belief and folk customs in the screenplay. Was this a film that fetishized or critiqued Ukrainian backwardness? The problem for these Muscovites was that they could not tell the difference. Nonetheless, the screenplay passed through both republican and central institutions, and entered into production in the summer of 1963.

The larger issue on the set involved a conflict between the director and the cinematographer. Paradjanov complained to Luhovs'kyi of Illienko's stubborn and disobedient character from the very beginning of production, nicknaming the cinematographer 'the Tank'. For his part, Illienko insisted upon an authorial role in the production, questioning Paradjanov: 'Who am I in this film? A cinematographer or [just] an obedient photographer?' (Luhovs'kyi 1998: 67–69). While on location, Paradjanov would get constantly distracted, sometimes disappearing from the set to pursue his own personal interests in Carpathian antiquities, and then taking offence at any suggestion that he should have alerted the crew to his absence. Many in the crew were apprehensive about these antics, along with his tyrannical style. Paradjanov and Illienko were increasingly at odds with each other during the summer and autumn of 1963. The latter, along with Kadochnikova, refused to work at one point after Paradjanov left the set in anger (Luhovs'kyi 1998: 73–75). In October, the studio blamed the director for 'coarse and untactful [...] accusations against the entire crew', but complied with his wish to replace Illienko with his friend and fellow Armenian, cinematographer Suren Shakhbazian (TsDAMLMU 670/1/1645: 174–75). Moreover, Paradjanov charged Luhovs'kyi with finding a replacement for Kadochnikova. The director and cinematographer later made up, and Illienko and Kadochnikova returned to the set at the end of October (Luhovs'kyi 1998: 75–77). But studio authorities and older film-makers at the studio continually accused Paradjanov of rude behaviour toward his cast and crew. At the end of his life, Illienko (2008b: 83–84) still harboured resentment about the way Paradjanov handled himself on the set, writing in his memoirs that he directed the film in a completely unprofessional manner and was 'captive to his studio aesthetic of a camera sick with cerebral palsy'. The cinematographer likened the relationship to a duel, which Paradjanov eventually

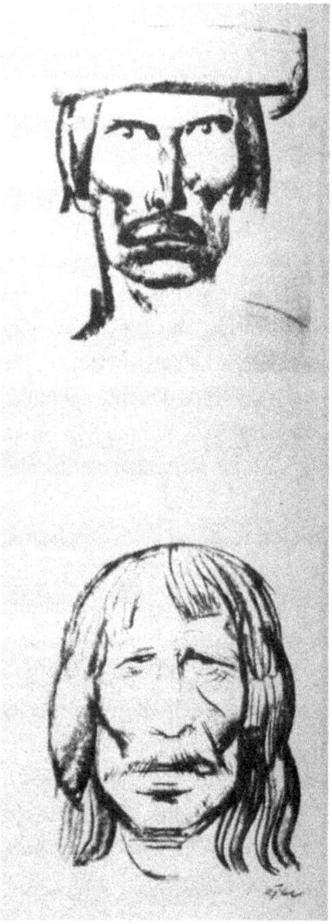

Figure 1: Iakutovych's sketches of Hutsul faces. From *Novyny kinoekrana*, 5 (1965).

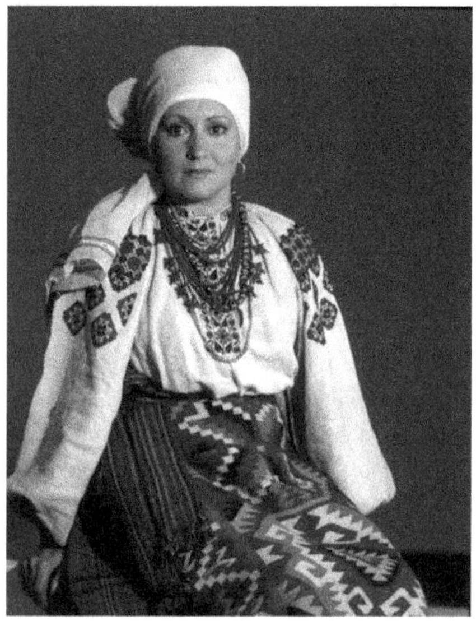

Figure 2: Larisa Kadochnikova in Ukrainian folk costume. Courtesy of the Aleksandr Dovzhenko National Centre, Kyiv.

won (2008b: 83–84).[7] Nonetheless, as we will see in the next chapter, Illienko's frantic camerawork, the likes of which Paradjanov hated, dominates the finished product.

Paradjanov's preference for Russian actors from Moscow also angered the studio leadership and the older Ukrainians working at the studio. After all, they now considered *Shadows* to be part of a larger Ukrainian cultural revival, and expected the film not only to improve the reputation of the 'made in Ukraine' label, but also to be made *by* Ukrainians. With the studio's blessing (and possibly a little coercion), Paradjanov had assembled a certifiably 'Ukrainian' crew, but continued to associate professional acting with Moscow. During production, the Ukrainian Film-makers' Union griped that the actress Kadochnikova of the Moscow Art Theatre (Moskovskii khudozhestvennyi akademicheskii teatr) was playing Marichka and the established Russian-Georgian actress Tat'iana Bestaeva played Palahna (TsDAMLMU 655/1/245).[8] Moreover, Paradjanov initially supported the actor from Mosfilm, Gennadii Iukhtin, to play Ivanko before Viktor Ivchenko, dean of the nascent Ukrainian film school, asked him to consider the Carpathian native, Ivan Mykolaichuk, for the role.[9]

In dispute with many at the studio and in his crew, Paradjanov insisted on shooting most of the film on location in the Carpathian villages of Verkhovyna, Bystrytsia, Sokolivka and Kryvorivnia, the area of Bukovina along the

Ukrainian-Romanian border usually called Hutsulshchyna, or 'the land of the Hutsuls'. For the mountain scenes, the crew contracted a local collective farm to build a road through a remote valley, with progress slower than anticipated and the meagre budget of 375,000 roubles already mostly spent. The production was consistently behind schedule and over-budget during the winter and spring of 1964, owing to delays in road construction and Mykolaichuk's overextended schedule. He was also playing Ukrainian national poet Taras Shevchenko in Volodymyr Denysenko's *Son/A Dream* (1964), which the studio still privileged over *Shadows*. At one point, Tsvirkunov forced Paradjanov to suspend production until the actor finished his role in the Shevchenko biopic, a film that almost no one saw. Even though Paradjanov completed the film in September, it would take another year before the film made it to the big screen.

Throughout the process of discussing and evaluating first the screenplay and then the rushes, misunderstandings (and outright condemnations) about the intention of this all-important and culturally sensitive film emerged. In the summer of 1964, even Oleksandr Syzonenko and Vasyl' Zemliak, both supporters of the film, complained of the 'ethnographic elements', even as they praised the film's 'correct interpretation' of Kotsiubyns'kyi. The seeming dissonance between such complaints and such praise lie in the purpose and style of Soviet literary adaptation, which expected not mere verisimilitude to the classical source, but also a harnessing of its political and ideological potential. The virtue of Paradjanov's film also seemed to be its problem: Kotsiubyns'kyi's novella was not readily available for a socialist-realist interpretation, nor did it conform to stereotypes of Ukrainians as the simple-minded, sing-songy 'Little Russians'[10] popularized in Stalinist cinema and widely understood by Soviet audiences through generic conventions.

Nonetheless, the studio watched a rough cut of the film in 1964, and most of the attendees were astounded by what they saw. While Ivanov and Tsvirkunov both expressed doubts about the exotic elements that appeared to fetishize Hutsul backwardness, most commented positively on the director's 'feel for ethnography and folklore', vindicating his 'poetic' approach to the subject matter. The establishment screenwriter Kostiantyn Kudiievs'kyi, who wrote popular war films for the studio, commented that the film demanded a 'great celebration' at the studio, indicating the importance of sophisticated films dedicated to Ukrainian subject matter for the studio's new branding (TsDAMLMU, 670/1/1750: 81–121).

Yet the studio's ambivalence about *Shadows* indicated how the film straddled a fine line between the acceptable expression of a Ukrainian identity during the 1960s and the auteurist principles of the Soviet Thaw on the one hand; and a nationalistic text that could aggravate Ukrainian-Russian relations and a complete refutation of the socialist realism canon on the other. After all, Paradjanov openly rejected the plot-centred vision of narrative cinema, and celebrated ethnographic spectacle, although not for a nationalistic purpose, Ukrainian or otherwise. Instead, the director foregrounded beauty for its own sake, and harnessed the symbols and metaphors in Hutsul folklore to speak to large philosophical questions. In many ways, this too constituted Mykhailo Kotsiubyns'kyi's vision for his novella, although, as we will see, the political stakes for such apolitical musings were a lot higher for Paradjanov.

Chapter 3
Film analysis

One of the keys to understanding Paradjanov's *Shadows of Forgotten Ancestors* lies in its eclectic mix of traditional literary sensibilities, surrealism and a documentary-like attention to ethnography. Through the use of subjective cinematography, location shooting, diegetic sound, and elements of ethnic texture and material culture that include folk costumes, religious icons, musical instruments, tools and other trinkets, the film constructs an authentic yet anachronistic space. Paradjanov carefully studied Hutsul marriage and funeral customs, material culture and folklore, in addition to the Carpathian landscape, architecture and even local hairstyles, before beginning the production (Luhovs'kyi 1998: 71). These qualities, along with the deep, hyper-saturated colour scheme – achieved by exploiting the unique but often poor qualities of Soviet-made Shostka film stock – make *Shadows* a rare and exceptionally beautiful viewing experience that holds hidden gems for audiences even after several views.

INFLUENCES, THEMES AND AUTHORSHIP

While *Shadows of Forgotten Ancestors* remains a wholly original and unique work of cinema, its authors – Paradjanov and Illienko in particular – were influenced by a range of classic Soviet auteurs, as well as more contemporary West European and Soviet film-makers. In his sole work of film theory, 'Vechnoe dvizhenie'/'Eternal Motion' (Paradzhanov 1966), along with his few public statements about the film, Paradjanov also acknowledged influence from Renaissance and Modernist painting, along with contemporary trends in Ukrainian poetry. During a rare moment of humility, he told his colleagues in 1966: 'Seven years ago [...] I couldn't do what I wanted to. I didn't know how. I was less literate. Today, when there's Fellini, Illienko, there's *Father of a Soldier* [Chkheidze, 1964], when there are five to six great poets in Ukraine [...]. I understand how to begin making new films at the studio' (TsDAMLMU 1127/1/172: 64). And although Illienko wrote and spoke much more about his art over the course of his life, we get no consistent sense of his influences, more often attributing his cinematographic style simply to personal authorship rather than a response to specific artistic stimuli.

His assistant director, Volodymyr Luhovs'kyi (1998: 61), wrote that the key to Paradjanov's film theory lies in his preference for spectacle over the psychological depth of the characters. While such typical statements about Paradjanov's aesthetic sensibilities certainly ring true in the many instances of decontextualized ethnographic tableaux in *Shadows*, we should also acknowledge the film's careful attention to epic form. Paradjanov's treatment of Ivanko's development from childhood to adulthood and then to his death remains a psychological exploration, even if the protagonist's actions and the succulent imagery are not always motivated by the plot. In *Shadows*, psychology and narrative are wed to what Kristin Thompson (1986: 130) has called 'excess', but the former is far from absent. Thompson (1986: 134) defines 'excess' as those elements that lie outside of the structures that unify the work, and the 'material of the image in film [that] creates a play which goes beyond this unity'. While classic narrative cinema tends to minimize excess by making the visual material as narratively motivated as possible and thus unobtrusive, Paradjanov tends to foreground visual style in his work, and the spectator must thereby contend with its excess.

In 'Eternal Motion', however, Paradjanov begins with an influence closer to home: quoting his VGIK professor, the Stalin-era Ukrainian film-maker Igor' Savchenko, he writes that directors needed to 'think with associations'. Instead of the unstructured associational 'play' of Thompson's 'excess', Savchenko's quote suggests an Eisenstein-inspired montage, where meaning is encoded into definitive juxtapositions and clear symbols: the slaughter of the cow at the end of *Stachka/Strike* (1924); the swan on the dying mother's belt buckle in *Bronenosets Potemkin/Battleship Potemkin* (1925); and the white horse hanging from the bridge during the July Days in *Oktiabr'/October* (1928) – these all provide examples of the kind of associational poetics (unusual for classical narrative cinema) that nonetheless directly support the plot. Paradjanov certainly employs such associations in *Shadows*. Yet he also juxtaposes images with objects that defy easy association, instead suggesting a surrealist dissonance between them. Paradjanov's use of montage does not always aim for clear associations, but often serves as a gallery of beautiful images.

After all, he moves from the lessons of Savchenko in 'Eternal Motion' to a very different affirmation about his 'passion for painting', writing that he 'perceives the frame as a self-contained canvas' (Paradzhanov 1966: 60). In this respect, he breaks from the main exemplars of Thaw cinema with their emphasis on narrative subtlety, psychological complexity and preference for monochrome. 'Colourlessness', as he called it, is 'portable' rather than specific. Instead, film-makers needed to study painters like the Dutch Renaissance master Pieter Bruegel the Elder (1525–69), the Japanese proto-impressionist Ogata Kōrin (1658–1716), Russian Wanderers Abram Arkhipov (1862–1930) and Mikhail Nesterov (1862–1942), and Cubists Fernand Léger (1881–1955) and Diego Rivera (1886–1957). He writes: 'For them, colour was not only a mood, added emotion, but a part of the content' (Paradzhanov 1966: 66). Unlike contemporary trends in film-making, where black-and-white images take us inside the lives and thoughts of the characters, Paradjanov asserts here that colour itself becomes the depth and substance of the image. Sviatoslav Ivanov (1973: 234) had a different take on Paradjanov's use of colour, writing in his 1973 dissertation on Ukrainian cinema in the 1960s and 1970s that 'colour exerts its own powerful dramaturgy' in the film. In fact, the film is largely structured around different colour schemes. Paradjanov and his crew shot most of the beginning of the film outside in nature, and these scenes consist of hues of greens, browns and white, signifying the consummation of Ivanko and Marichka's ideal love. The middle of the film, in the chapter 'Loneliness', shifts to black and white to reflect Ivanko's darkened soul after Marichka dies. Finally, the third section of the film is dominated by red, orange and yellow, suggesting the carnal rather than natural love of Palahna. Moreover, this final colour scheme serves as a premonition of Ivanko's death through its association with blood and the red-tinted fade at the end of each chapter. Thus, colour becomes at once a static and painterly canvas to reveal the beauty of the image, as well as a dynamic function of the plot.

A second theme that Paradjanov discusses in 'Eternal Motion' is his interest in Ukrainian folklore. Here we see his influence from not only his professor, Savchenko, but also from Aleksandr Dovzhenko himself. From the late 1920s until the end of his career in the late 1940s, Dovzhenko made extensive use of folkloric tropes and, at least his early Ukrainian films, are rich in ethnographic details about peasant life. After Kiev Studios renamed itself after Dovzhenko in 1958, Ukrainian film-makers were keen to demonstrate their affinity for folklore as 'heirs to Dovzhenko' (Stankevych 1964: 3). Unlike many of his colleagues at the studio though, for Paradjanov folklore takes on not only an ahistorical quality, but also something that is at once mobile and specific, rather than 'hollowly national' in orientation. And while his knowledge of Ukrainian folklore came to him from the visual arts through painters like Fedir Manailo, graphic artists like Heorhii Iakutovych and film-makers like Dovzhenko and Savchenko, it also emerged from his reading of Modernist and contemporary Ukrainian literature.

Significantly, Paradjanov considered his film to be a legitimate cinematic adaptation of Kotsiubyns'kyi's folkloric style and content, even if the film was unusual as a Soviet adaptation. He found in the novella an amalgamation of Ukrainian folklore and ethnography with painterly and poetic forms, and claimed to have been attracted to the 'pure sense of beauty, the harmony, and infinity. The feeling of that point where nature becomes art and art becomes nature'

(Paradzhanov 1966: 62). In Kotsiubyns'kyi's literary style, colour and excess are embedded in his use of metaphor, which frequently functions intertextually by reference to visual forms: 'The entire world was like a fairy tale' (Kotsiubyns'kyi 1967: 9), he writes at the beginning of the novella, more likely an allusion to the contemporaneous Symbolist paintings of fairy tales from artists like Mikhail Vrubel' than to the oral or written texts themselves.

As Paradjanov would be in his adaptation, so was Kotsiubyns'kyi concerned with the verbal and aural ethnoscape of the Carpathians. In both the novella and the film, folk songs and gossip function for exposition in the absence of extensive dialogue. Here, emphasis lies on the sound, texture and rhythm of the Hutsul dialect, what Ol'ha Briukhovets'ka (2002: 29) calls 'improper direct speech' – i.e. speech directed at the audience but which is not meant to be entirely understood. In Kotsiubyns'kyi, the language of the narration conveys the confusion of narrative voice. He uses the term *bovhar* instead of the standard Ukrainian *pastukh* for cowherd, and *buryshka* instead of *kartoplia* for potato, as well as many other non-standard Ukrainian words. The end of the story included a glossary of terms to help the reader of standard Ukrainian understand the text, but the refusal to translate these terms within the text itself was a significant authorial decision, which sought to convey the ethnoscape of the narrative. Kotsiubyns'kyi's language functioned on the level of 'colour' in that it sought to convey a spectacle beyond the direct capabilities of a literary text, and this allowed Paradjanov to claim that he was remaining true to the original while indulging his interest in a painterly and poetic cinema. In this respect, too, he claims at once to fulfil his duty for literary verisimilitude and authentic ethnographic representation while possessing a licence to divert from such precision when art demands it.

One of those diversions lies in the representation of the film's protagonist, Ivanko. Whereas Kotsiubyns'kyi imagines the hero as completely enmeshed within the cyclical Hutsul world of spirits, divination, holidays, labour and death, Paradjanov's Ivanko is a quintessentially 'modernist hero' (Briukhovets'ka 2002: 29). He 'represents the traditional community, the animism and demonology of the Hutsuls', but also 'the essence of the modern, the almost existential personalism, a tragic self-consciousness' (2002: 29). Many critics and scholars during the Thaw itself identified the theme of Ivanko's individuality in tension with the everyday life in Hutsulshchyna (for instance, Anninskii 1971; Solov'eva and Shitova 1989; Turbin 1964, 1965). More recently, Levon Grigorian (2011: 95–115) has suggested that the main theme of the film is Ivanko's failed attempts to escape fate, which we might read as the essence of the Hutsuls' cyclical existence. The theme of the individual and what literary critic Ivan Dziuba (1989: 67) called the 'singularity of a great love, the irretrievable loss of the ideal' represented by childhoodwere common tropes in the literary culture of the Soviet 1950s and 1960s. These themes appeared front and centre in Paradjanov's adaptation, and were well represented in the poetry of Ivan Drach, a good friend of the director's and a literary consultant on the set.

Other elements also point toward the profound literary basis of Paradjanov's film, not least of which is the division of the film into chapters (a convention that Tarkovsky would also employ in *Andrei Rublev* [1966] the following year), and the frequent use of direct quotes from Kotsiubyns'kyi's novella in the form of intertitles. Another major theme in the film, which is not only lifted from the literary source, but also present in other *fin-de-siècle* Ukrainian classics such as Lesia Ukrainka's *Lisova pisnia/The Forest Song* (1912), is the contrast between 'sacred and profane love'. The theme is represented by the two women in Ivanko's life, which Dziuba (1989: 67) traces back to Renaissance artist Titian's famous painting of the same title from 1517, thus returning us to Paradjanov's interest in classical and biblical themes. The latter permeate the film's metaphorical and symbolic universe, with frequent allusions to Greek mythology and the Gospels.

Contemporary trends in cinematography, editing and *mise-en-scène* round out the final influence on *Shadows of Forgotten Ancestors*. Paradjanov's film emerged at the cusp of a radical transformation of film-making in Western Europe that rejected Hollywood's influence and other native traditions. This transformation is usually identified with the French New Wave, as well as other movement cinemas like Italian neorealism, New German Cinema and so-called auteur cinema (the idea that cinematic meaning emerges from the choices of a director-artist) more generally.

Paradjanov and Illienko's connection to this transformation resists an easy explanation. On the one hand, Paradjanov flaunted his connections with West European film-makers, with visitors to his apartment shown letters that Federico Fellini had sent him and gifts he received from French New Wave film composer Michel Legrand (Luhovs'kyi 1998: 25). Fellini, whose *Otto e mezzo/8 ½* (1963) had just won the Grand Prix at the Third Moscow International Film Festival, was widely popular in the Soviet Union at the time, and his absurd style of narration in the latter film and his interest in unusual theatrics in films like *La Strada/The Road* (1954) would have sat nicely with Paradjanov's own ideas about the cinema. Moreover, Illienko's jerky, handheld camera that fluidly shifts between objective and subjective points of view, as well as the film's frequent use of jump cuts point toward the direct influence of the New Wave. In *Shadows*, for example, we see frequent violations of classical form in the film's expressive montage, which consists of cuts that do not match the action, along with successive shots that cut to the same action or image merely at a different focal length or distance from the action or image. Robert Lakatosh (1999) argues that *Shadows* also contains a kind of 'synthetic', 'imperfect' montage during its action sequences (the search for Marichka's body; Ivanko's funeral, etc.), which is more characteristic of documentary in its attempts to include only important information and remove excessive material. Moreover, the use of expressive and synthetic montage serves to 'deepen the otherness of the world we are shown' (1999: 3).

Jean-Luc Godard's *À bout de souffle/Breathless* (1960) and Jean Rouch's *Chronique d'un été/Chronicle of a Summer* (1960) popularized such camera and editing techniques, but neither of these 'decadent' films were purchased by Goskino for screening in the Soviet Union (Baskakov 1996: 134). Nonetheless, many Soviet film-makers active during the 1960s and 1970s now remember seeing French New Wave films either while studying at VGIK, Moscow's Cinema House, or the film archive (Gosfil'mofond) outside of Moscow in Belye Stolby. Other directors and critics remember that they saw some of the films from the French New Wave at international film festivals in Cannes and Karlovy Vary. Many of them claim, however, that the influence of the French New Wave was far overshadowed by that of Italian neorealism during the Thaw (Trofimenkov 1999). Illienko was studying at VGIK during the heyday of the French New Wave when Claude Chabrol, François Truffaut and Jean-Luc Godard all released their debut films (1958–1960), and so he would have undoubtedly seen them all. Paradjanov, on the other hand, lived in Kiev from 1952 until 1966, where film-makers constantly complained of their limited access to artistically significant foreign films (TsDAMLMU, 670/1/2159: 74, 76; 655/1/446: 7–8; 655/1/450: 83). Moreover, Paradjanov much preferred the static camera, long takes and tableaux framing that would characterize his next two films – the unfinished *Kyivs'ki fresky/Kyiv Frescoes* (1966) and *Tsvet granata/The Colour of Pomegranates* (1968) – rather than the frantic, New Wave-inspired style at work in most of *Shadows*.

Nonetheless, Illienko never claimed a foreign source either, largely because he possessed a usable domestic influence in Mikhail Kalatozov's cinematographer, Sergei Urusevskii (Illienko 1972: 128).[11] While the cinematography in Kalatozov's famous *Letiat zhuravli/The Cranes are Flying* (1956) utilized smooth tracking shots, his next film, *Neotpravlennoe pis'mo/The Letter Never Sent* (1959), shares a number of traits with Illienko's work on *Shadows*, including frequent use of a handheld camera and low-angle shots. Even here, however, Urusevskii's work appears as controlled chaos in comparison to Illienko's experimental shots that seamlessly blend subjective point-of-view (POV) with objective narration, and distort space by rarely employing eye-level shots. In *Shadows*, Illienko often uses the camera as a character within the film's diegetic space, thus evoking Italian film-maker Pier Paolo Pasolini's (2001: 48, 51) notion of a 'cinema of poetry', wherein the 'camera [is] felt' (Briukhovets'ka 2002: 29). In the end, Illienko (1972: 128) claims no influence at all and told the journal *Iskusstvo kino/Cinema Art* in 1972 that the methods for making *Shadows* were just 'in the air'. He said much the same to Ukrainian-Canadian film scholar Bohdan Nebesio (1994: 47): 'I wanted to absorb everything around me. And I began to experiment with a hand-held camera striving in some way to imitate a whirlpool which draws everything into it'. Here again, content may have dictated form, as the spontaneous camera reflected the spontaneity of Hutsul life, in contrast to Paradjanov's static aesthetic that strives toward conveying beauty directly to the viewer.

The influences on *Shadows of Forgotten Ancestors* are thus varied, complex and difficult to pin down. Paradjanov's preference for a painterly *mise-en-scène* defies easy categorization as either traditionalist or Modernist; his interest in folklore and ethnography resists both a Soviet patriotic function and a Ukrainian nationalist understanding, even though he (probably more so than Illienko) knew the literary canon upon which such nationalism rested; and Illienko's cinematography is simultaneously derivative of recent cinematographic trends and wholly unique to his developing ideas as an artist. Finally, despite my attempts to determine plausible explanations for the complex symbolism and associations contained in *Shadows of Forgotten Ancestors*, we should remember that Paradjanov's intentions were always fairly loose and assumed a certain flexibility in interpretation.

INTRODUCTORY SEQUENCE: IVANKO AND MARICHKA'S CHILDHOOD

This unusual and oftentimes inexplicable film begins with an explanation. White letters on a black background inform us: 'This film is a poetic drama about the love of Ivan and Marichka. The film takes us into the world of the folk tales, customs and everyday life of old Carpathia'. Such an explanatory title, archaic in form in its allusions to the conventions of silent cinema, fulfilled the demand from Goskino for a clearer exposition. According to Robert Payne (1990: 35), the intertitle, with its direct reference to Kotsiubyns'kyi, self-consciously 'reminds the viewer that the film is a textualizing construct, an artifact situated in a specific history'. In this case, the film's tagline is incorporated into the titles themselves, which identifies the plot and setting directly. As the title and production credits fill the screen with dark red block letters on a black background, we hear an axe chopping wood. The colour red permeates *Shadows of Forgotten Ancestors*, not only because of its association with blood and mortality, but also for its presence within Hutsul material culture. Viewers are immediately disoriented as the credits fade to an exterior close-up of a young boy, Ivanko, his angelic face staring upward. Such direct exposition was not unusual for Soviet films set in exotic locales like the Carpathian Mountains. Viktor Ivanov's Ukrainian film *Oleksa Dovbush* (1960), about an eighteenth-century Hutsul freedom fighter, employed a similar method when it opened with a narrator telling us over a view of a mountain vista:

> The Carpathian Mountains, like deep wrinkles in the ancient face of the land. From time immemorial, children of the one mother of Ukraine lived here until the Polish, Austrian, Hungarian, and Wallachian lords seized this land, tore it to pieces, and divided it among themselves [...]. Anger was excavated from the hearts of the people [...]. Two hundred years ago, this anger had a human name. They called him Oleksa Dovbush...
>
> (TsDAMLMU, 670/2/1536: 2)[12]

Ivanov's direct exposition both serves to provide a correct historical interpretation of the plot, and familiarizes the landscape for spectators. In contrast, Paradjanov juxtaposes direct exposition with a disorienting close-up that rejects the convention of an establishing shot. As Inna Solov'eva and Vera Shitova (1989: 86) argue, the aesthetic of the mountain vista is precisely what Kotsiubyns'kyi suggests in his novella, and which Paradjanov soundly rejects in his focus on faces and objects.

Ivanko calls out to a different Oleksa, and we see an abrupt cut to a medium shot in which a jerky handheld camera follows the boy in profile on a forested downward mountain slope. The forest is silent except for the sound of chopping wood and snow crunching under Ivanko's feet. 'Oleksa, do you hear me?' he calls out a second time. The boy pulls out a piece of bread from his bag and yells out: 'Come and eat!' He waves the bread in the air, and the film cuts to a close-up of a twenty-something man, with a typically Hutsul hairstyle – short fringe and longer straight hair on the sides and back – and a large moustache. He begins waving his arms frantically and shouts: 'Listen! Run,

Ivanko!' The film cuts to one of its more remarkable shots: the camera, seemingly from the point of view of a falling tree, comes down on the unsuspecting boy's head. Oleksa runs into the shot, sparing his brother's life and sacrificing his own. Time is sped up at the last moment, resembling primitive stop-motion animation, as we see the older brother's look of frantic terror before the tree/camera crashes down on him. Oleksa has been killed both literally and symbolically.

'Eternal Motion' contains a sustained critique of the inauthenticity and artistic mistakes in Ivanov's film. The Carpathian nature, which in *Oleksa Dovbush* personifies the people's resistance, is understood here as its oppressor, having the power over life and death.

The scene cuts to Ivanko in medium shot, begging his lifeless brother to let go of him. There seems to be a short delay in action between this shot and the previous one, as the cut does not appear to match the action. The camera moves up unsteadily in an arcing fashion, resembling the opening shot of Kalatozov's *The Letter Never Sent*, as Ivanko continues to tug at Oleksa's arm. From directly overhead, we look down at Ivanko as he finally frees himself from his brother's deathly grip. He runs off-camera to the sound of a loud horn called a *trembita*, the most iconic of Hutsul instruments. While resembling the more common Swiss alphorn, and used for the similar purpose of calling highland communities together for weddings, funerals and other events, the *trembita* lacks the curved, flared end that rests on the ground, and is played instead by pointing it upward. By the mid-1960s, *trembitary* [*trembita* players] were part of folk music ensembles that performed professionally. Here, as elsewhere in the film, Paradjanov uses the sound of the instrument to denote death, even as the image of the *trembitar* functions as ethnographic colour. The camera, now looking at the lifeless Oleksa from overhead, swerves slightly, and slowly spins around. Illienko will use this device continually to indicate the passage from life to death, or other emotionally laden changes. Finally, the scene cuts to Ivanko stumbling down the mountain. The camera follows him as before, with many trees partially obscuring the action, making viewers aware of the camera's presence. A fade to red follows as the *trembita* continues to blast. The dual function of the *trembita* to signal both birth and death reveals one of the film's cyclical structures, and Illienko's camera further underscores this structure with his spinning camera. We should not fail to notice Ivanko's exceptionality in this opening scene, as Oleksa very consciously sacrifices his own life for his brother's. Moreover, the prolonged period that we watch the boy struggle to free himself from death's grip underscores and foreshadows Ivanko's fate.

This first scene, which serves as a cold opening, contrasts sharply with the archaic introductory title, the latter of which substitutes for an establishing shot. Illienko shot the scene almost entirely in close-up, with only two medium shots to orient the viewer toward a particular place (i.e. a high altitude) and time (i.e. winter). The camera shifts between static and traditional shots to the shaky movement of a documentarian, and then to the viewpoint of objects in nature, trees and perhaps even the wind, which possess a certain consciousness in both the novella and Paradjanov's adaptation.

The red intertitle obliquely references the Kotsiubyns'kyi centenary, and then offers a quote from the author, also archaic in its reference to silent cinema: 'The Carpathians, land of the Hutsuls, forgotten by God and man'. The uncanny sound of the *trembita* fades to familiar church bells. A visual fade reveals the first long shot in the film: three figures – Ivanko and his parents – plant a cross for Oleksa on the top of a snowy hill. We hear a voice-over of Ivanko's mother (played by Stalin-era actress Nina Alisova, who was Kadochnikova's real-life mother), who utters the prayer: 'Oleksa my darling. Your suffering is my own. Dear God, preserve Ivanko, my last child'. Such expository voice-over also functions as interior monologue, as words that could have been spoken aloud but instead recede into the auditory shadows. Illienko uses a long lens in this shot, which flattens the space, making it appear two-dimensional, before the camera pans down to two figures on horseback. As Ivanko walks down the hill, he appears to pop out of the shot as the horse exits the frame, and we shift from a painterly space to a cinematic one. The voice-over fades out as we hear the sounds of a man chanting a haunting lamentation, which will be repeated toward the end of the film. The words, however, resist any simple connection to the story:

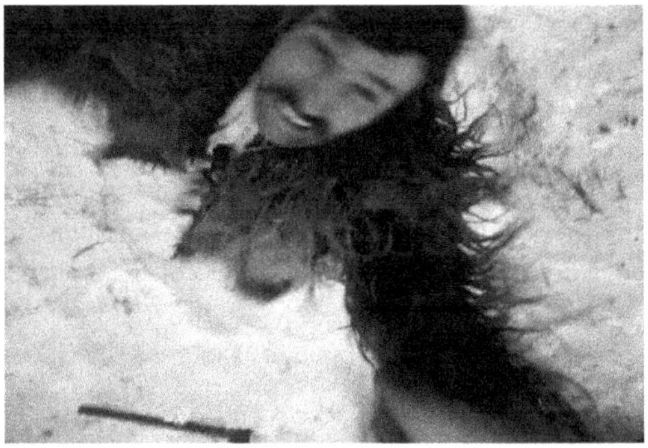

Figure 3: The tree falls on Oleksa. Still from the film.

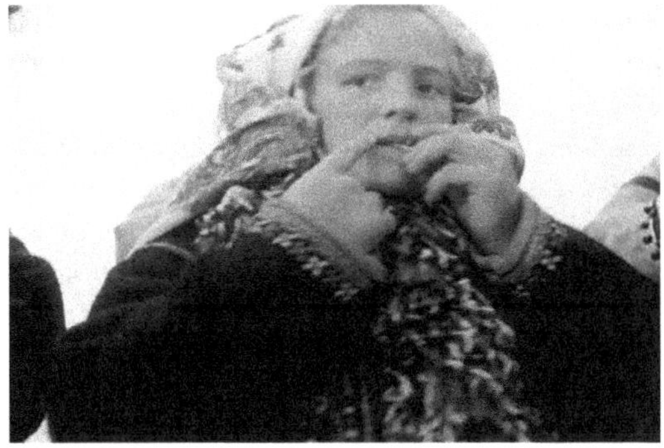

Figure 4: *Drymba* player. Still from the film.

Oh, a cuckoo sang,
And it will sing.
And I want to tell the truth
About days long ago.
There were giants,
They walked for miles.
They almost could reach
The heavens with their hands.
And their wives were with them…

The first two lines about the cuckoo reappear in other songs throughout the film, as well as in Kotsiubyns'kyi, and seem to function as a call to the community to gather and listen. The subsequent reference to *liudy-velykany* ['giants'], however, is absent from the novella and suggests instead Greco-Roman mythology, its rendition here within a Hutsul folkloric manner an attempt to read Ivanko's story deep within the story's allegorical framework.

The film cuts to a close-up of a peasant woman playing a type of mouth harp that the highlanders call a *drymba*, which makes an odd percussive twanging sound using the finger of one hand and contorting one's mouth in different shapes. Viewers might recognize the instrument from John Ford's *Young Mr. Lincoln* (1939), in which the hero demonstrates his small-town authenticity by playing an Appalachian version of it. Here, however, the jerky handheld camera disrupts the bucolic landscape, while maintaining the close-up as it moves left to reveal two other peasants playing the same instrument. Viewers appear to be aligned with Ivanko's point of view in this shot, as if members of an audience watching a folk music ensemble, until the boy seemingly pops into the frame at the end of the line, revealing a subjective yet extra-diegetic origin to the shot. Ivanko turns away from them in close-up, and the camera moves on, jerking away so rapidly that we see an impressionistic blur of colours as three women wave shawls in the air. The camera, moving faster, pauses upon a freakish-looking man in mangled wool jangling some metal objects that hang from a roughly-constructed wooden frame. He smiles maniacally as the camera quickly moves on to three men (once again) on an incline, also ringing bells.

Where are we in this scene? A village market morphs into a human zoo for tourists to gawk at the local Carpathian colour. Such an Orientalizing gaze is confirmed by Paradjanov's December 1964 statements to an audience of his colleagues in Moscow when he said: 'Such barbarism happens in the centre of Europe, between Uzhhorod and Chernivtsi' (RGALI 2936/1/528: 43). The viewer is exposed to sensory overload as the camera jerks away abruptly, mimicking our distracted attention. We focus once again on a single old man in close-up, holding several staffs, before moving on. Two men carry limp lambs around their necks, a motif that returns several times throughout the film. A man and a woman, better dressed than the rest, hammer posts into the snowy ground. Another man plays a *foltar* [a local variant of a flute], with metal objects planted in the ground obscuring our view of him. Another man behind a kiosk sells ornamental objects and drinks vodka. A woman calls out, 'Toy horses, toy horses, toy horses!' Church bells are still ringing, but we do not know where they are coming from. Two poorly dressed men are fighting on the ground until one of them crawls toward the camera and bleats at us, telling us that the lambs are all gone. Hutsuls in the film frequently lament the loss of young livestock (lambs and kids in particular), which we might assume offers a metaphor initially for the deaths of Ivanko's many brothers, later for Marichka's lost child, and finally for Palahna's inability to conceive. Kiev literary scholar Vadym Skurativs'kyi offers another explanation, suggesting that such statements obliquely reference the collectivization of agriculture and the longer-term decline of the Ukrainian peasant (personal communication June 2006). Finally, Ivanko enters the frame from the right to reveal himself as the curious subject of the gaze. A quick camera movement to the right realigns us with Ivanko's point of view, and also divulges the hitherto unseen church's location. His mother, seen in medium shot, is in the middle of a group of praying women. She calls to him as the camera (from Ivanko's point of view) moves toward her, and she tells the perennial subject of the camera's gaze to 'stop looking' at the crazy man on the ground. Again, Ivanko enters the frame from the right and, within the same shot, the camera pauses in close-up of the mother and son. They enter the church and we finally cut to an interior shot. Throughout the previous shot, the peasants are communicating with the camera, at times revealed to be us, the viewer, and at other moments Ivanko.

Inside the church, the human zoo transforms into an ethnographic museum with traditional icons, crosses, religious books, candles and chanting. Ivanko emerges from the left of the frame, appearing as a casual observer rather than a participant in the ritual. The protagonist's separation from the community is striking, and allows us to identify with him immediately. Even the boy's physical appearance differs markedly from other Hutsuls. His brown hair, cut in a contemporary, urban style, and an unadorned white coat with a kerchief tied in the manner of a Young Pioneer sets him apart from the dark and elaborately costumed church-goers, thereby suggesting that he is not unlike the child of a typical Soviet spectator. Ivanko toys with a thick Bible and cross while his mother tries to reign in his tourist-like interest in the sacred objects on display. Eventually, a properly behaved little girl halts his progress, and Ivanko is forced to move behind an icon, which is surrounded by other little girls. We follow the absent-minded Ivanko to the right as men are lighting candles. He looks at them with a vague curiosity. A cut takes us to a close-up of two women and a man collecting offerings. The camera follows the man to the back of the congregation as he collects coins from worshipers. He stops at Ivanko, now standing next to his father, a wizened moustachioed Hutsul, as they turn around to make an offering.

At this moment, the scene's pace shifts as Illienko's mobile, observational camera cuts to Ivanko in close-up and then to a reverse shot of an icon with an angel fighting Satan. Such classical methods signal the film's first plot point. Ivanko's father, Petro, appears in close-up, and introduces the rivalry with the Hutentiuk family as a social conflict between rich and poor: 'You won't find Satan in church. Satan is among men. See? He gives money to God but cheats the poor'. Looking to his left, a low-angled close-up reveals the Hutentiuk patriarch, Onufrii, placing money on the plate. The man appears grotesque and portly, with oiled hair, a moustache and dressed in a colourful *serdak* [a short Hutsul overcoat]. His eyes move left and right to make sure others can see him playing with coins before tossing them onto the offering plate. The film cuts away to the plate and then to a close-up of Paliichuk laughing. The film's interpretation of the family feud as social in origin breaks from Kotsiubyns'kyi and presents one of the few nods to socialist realism. The novella imagined the conflict in line with the Capulets and Montagues, as an age-old feud fuelled by murder and revenge.

After Petro's rude laughter, the film then cuts away to a medium shot of two identical men at the altar, who look at each other simultaneously before looking away from the camera. The shot reveals Paradjanov's sense of the uncanny; a brief moment that draws our attention away from the narrative, but offers us nothing more than the beautiful symmetry that these human objects embody. Hutentiuk, in close-up, calls the Paliichuks 'paupers', telling them they

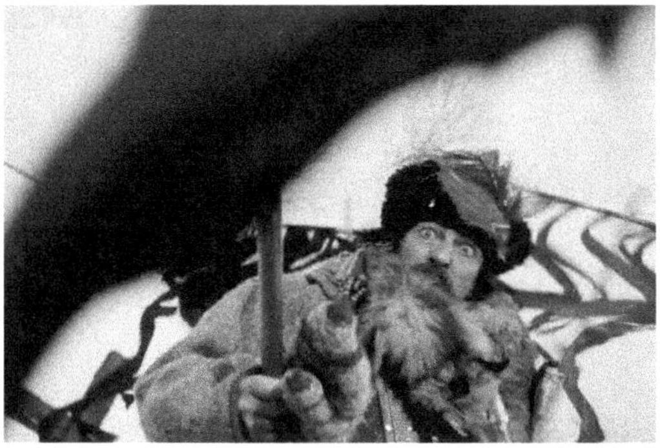

Figure 5: The frame drenched in blood. Still from the film.

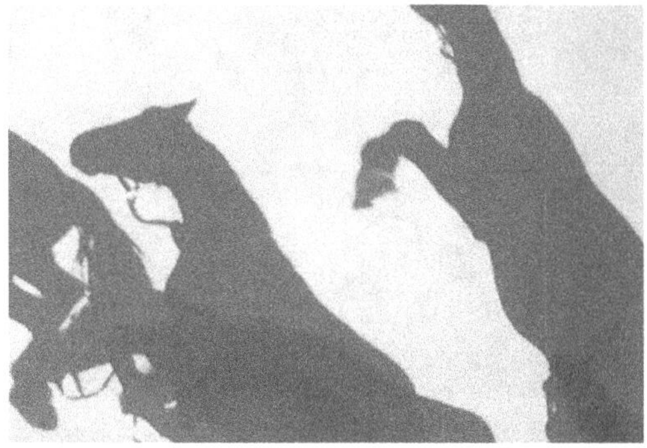

Figure 6: 'Wild Horses of Fire'. Still from the film.

do not belong inside the church. Each of these shots – Ivanko, Paliichuk, Hutentiuk, the offering plate and the men at the altar – is self-contained and exists outside the larger space of the church. Here, the film presents a deceptive mix of Eisenstein-inspired montage, and a spectacle of beautiful objects possessing their own aesthetic qualities apart from the overdetermined meaning contained in Paradjanov's archaic editing style. The plot itself functions as a red herring, diverting our attention away from, but also enticing us with, these human and static objects.

The exchange between the two men leads to a fight, as the film jumps in time to a crowded medium shot. Drawing on Gilles Deleuze, Robert Efird (2014: 29) calls this jump – typical for the film more generally – a 'break in the diegetic whole, [where] a deliberate and creative falsity creeps into the interval, which now, as much as the images themselves, acquires autonomous value in the disjunction between the successive shots'. Hutentiuk's wife joins the melee, while Ivanko's mother tries to prevent her husband from fighting. The tracking shot at the beginning of the scene now moves in reverse, as the two families leave the crowded church to continue the conflict outside. After a cut to an exterior shot, the camera follows Hutentiuk and his wife through the market scene described above. The camera shifts to the left: first to the crazed man still bleating like a goat, and then to the Paliichuks arguing. The camera moves again to the right and we notice that Ivanko's father has an axe in his hand. We follow Petro to the right as he lifts his axe; it continues to shift until Paliichuk is out of the frame, before it rests on a canted framing of Onufrii as he raises his own axe. He brings it down on the camera and blood enters the frame, partially obscuring the assailant who betrays a momentary look of surprise and regret. As in previous shots (although here most clearly), Illienko shifts between objective to subjective points of view without cutting.

The film then cuts to a red-tinted extreme low-angle shot of four horses jumping as church bells ring and a *trembita* blares. Levon Grigorian (2011: 97) implies that the horses serve a biblical function to carry the soul of Paliichuk from earth into heaven, although others have seen the scene in a more symbolic and metaphorical manner. Horses are frequent components in Ukrainian folklore, and also appear regularly in the early Ukrainian works of Nikolai Gogol and in Aleksandr Dovzhenko's films about Ukraine. According to the poet Ivan Drach, the horse reveals an 'opulent' nature that serves as a contrast to the Ukrainian peasant's 'savage fate' (TsDAMLMU 670/1/1781: 47). Thus, Paradjanov left the image unmotivated by the narrative, precisely because such a symbolic image was already overdetermined. Interestingly, *Shadows* was distributed abroad during the Soviet period with the title *Wild Horses of Fire*, which Sovexportfilm felt encapsulated the film's meaning (Ivanov 1973: 234).

We return to Ivanko in the midst of the pandemonium after the fight. He runs to the right as the camera follows in a fluid tracking shot, eventually finding the girl, Marichka, who had blocked his way in the church. Because she is Hutentiuk's daughter, Ivanko slaps her in the face, causing her to break down and cry. Some time has passed as the film cuts to a series of bushes, behind which Ivanko is chasing Marichka. In a long shot that resembles amateur

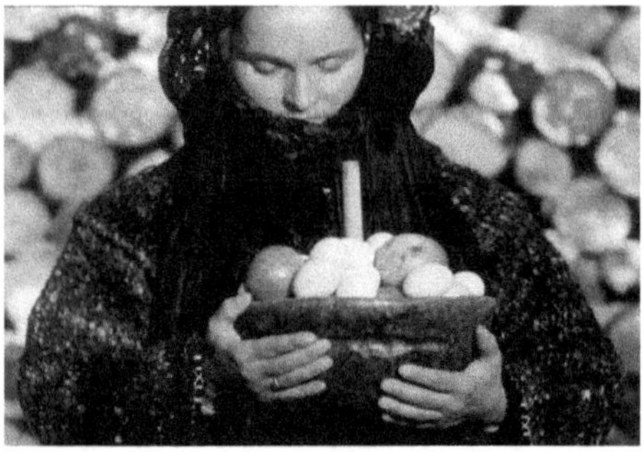

Figure 7: Ethnographic tableaux.
Still from the film.

footage, a handheld camera follows the two children running down a hill until the action stops next to a large river, the famed Cheremosh. The boy throws her elegant scarves in the river as Marichka struggles with him. Bragging, she tells him that she has better ones anyway. We see the two children in a medium shot facing each other. The boy's anger appears disingenuous, a mere pretext to flirt with the girl. After all, Ivanko remains the detached observer, even in the midst of his father's murder. After his scripted anger, he woos her by playing his *floiar*, but they continue to argue flirtatiously about who started the fight between their fathers. Finally, Marichka breaks down in tears again and Ivanko looks at her in his typically curious fashion. Rare for the film, Paradjanov tells the story of Ivanko and Marichka's burgeoning love in classical form, but refuses immediate resolution.

The next scene returns us to the spectacle of Hutsul religious ritual and material culture with a sequence of self-contained close-ups: religious banners on the ground; a young man staring at the camera; a woman with a bowl containing apples, potatoes and eggs; the alms collector who blows out a lantern; an old man with vodka; and a man holding a cross made out of birch trees. Women are chanting what appears to be a completely improvised song throughout this sequence, with different women singing it at their own paces. As such, the words are unintelligible.

Finally, Ivanko, the curious onlooker, watches the butts of two axes hammer a peg into his father's coffin. A *trembita* drowns out the chants as the film cuts to a handheld close-up of Ivanko's mother gesticulating and wailing. Finally, a white frame reveals a funeral procession in medium shot, as the participants emerge from behind a snow-covered hill. The man with the birch cross leads the procession. Several men with religious banners pass through the frame to reveal Petro's oxen-pulled coffin, as Ivanko's mother performs a scripted lament to her husband and vows revenge against the Hutentiuks. The *trembita* sounds again as Ivanko emerges into the frame, looking off to the right, distracted as usual. A line of *trembitary* plays as the boy descends the hill to find Marichka spying on the procession in the forest. They quickly run off together as a jerky handheld camera follows them to the right. Once again, we hear his mother's wailing in the background, and the camera shifts quickly to the left, the action blurred, and then a final a cut back to the procession from Ivanko's point of view. Ivanko runs into the frame and back to the procession as the film fades to red. The final scene of the film's first act reveals another archaism: the preliminary close-ups of people and objects serve an introductory function reminiscent of Eisenstein's 'montage of attractions'. The characters reveal themselves to us directly before Ivanko returns us to the plot. Like us, Ivanko too is a viewer, with his curious gaze; somehow separate from the ethnographic spectacle, but bound to his culture by nature.

'IVANKO AND MARICHKA'

Unlike Kotsiubyns'kyi's novella, Paradjanov's film is divided into chapters. We begin the first proper chapter, 'Ivanko and Marichka', with another expository intertitle, which tells us: 'The death of his father did not live as long in Ivanko's memory as the meeting with the girl…'. Taken directly from the novella, the intertitle signals the end of the explicitly social conflict between the Paliichuks and Hutentiuks. Although some Soviet commentators would continue to understand Ivanko as a member of the proletariat, the film no longer deviates from the novella solely to provide a social interpretation to the action (as it does in the introductory sequence). The first scene opens with numerous shots of the now adolescent children frolicking during the spring. In voice-over, Marichka chants a love song to Ivanko, with several lines appearing in Kotsiubyns'kyi's novella, while others appear in the film for the first time:

> Oh, a white sheep has run from the highland pasture,
> I love you, pretty beloved, and your pretty little words.
> And when the shepherds put their white sheep to pasture,
> They will put my little songs under their *kresani.*[13]
> Oh, a cuckoo sang and there is a river nearby,
> And who made these little songs? Ivanko's Marichka did.
> The wind blows from the highland pasture far above,
> There Ivanko's Marichka tends the sheep.
> Where should I hide you, my lovely little songs?
> Perhaps I shall sow you, my little songs, into the mountains…

Much as the previous chant about giants did, this song enshrines Marichka's and Ivanko's love into an allegorical and folkloric canon, initially 'hiding' it under a unique object of Hutsul material culture (the *kresania*) and finally within the eternal fabric of the landscape itself. In this latter respect, the song also evokes Aleksandr Dovzhenko's first major film, *Zvenyhora/Zvenigora* (1927), which revolves around a transhistorical search for the 'riches of Ukraine' hidden within the mythical mountain of the title. The hidden nature of the love/riches evinces its very power. Here, the reference to a cuckoo [*zosul'ka*] also reveals the power of that which is hidden, as it evokes the tale of Zeus' disguise as this bird to seduce Hera. Interestingly, Solov'eva and Shitova also reference a Greek source in the story of Ivanko and Marichka's budding childhood love. Rather than Romeo and Juliet, the second-century story of Daphnis and Chloe provides a more compelling source that considers the pastoral and erotic undertones that Paradjanov imparts to the childhood relationship (Solov'eva and Shitova 1989: 83–84).

The first lines, however, return us to the theme of a lost lamb: 'Oh, a white lamb ran from the highland pasture', suggesting a lost innocence, while the cuckoo also evokes fertility. However, Paradjanov drew these first lines from Kotsiubyns'kyi, so they may also refer to the writer's literary distinction between the top of the mountain (associated with divination and magic) and the valleys below (associated with worldly things like love and money) (Rubchak 1981). The children's love exists somewhere in between these spaces, both transcendent and of the material world. The earthy sound of an axe returns us to the Carpathian ethnoscape of the film. Ivanko plays his *floiar* and sings for the first time what will become a mantra, 'Where are my little goats [*kozy*][14]?' After hearing a howl, Marichka screams, first in fright and then in delight, as the children literally descend a mountain, in this case to swim naked in a creek. The sight of such nudity was quite unusual in Soviet cinema, either before or after 1964. Although Tarkovsky's *Andrei Rublev* would feature nudity in the chapter 'Holiday' during a paganistic celebration of St John's Eve, the sight of naked children in *Shadows* violated the puritanical image of them in Soviet cinema.

At one point in the descent, Illienko's shadow with the camera is clearly visible as it pans across the creek, making the agency of the film-makers most evident. This further suggests the blurring of subjective and objective narration, as well as that between documentary and fiction. At only fifteen minutes in to *Shadows of Forgotten Ancestors*, Paradjanov and his cast and crew have already revealed an eclectic catalogue of sources and influences, ranging from ancient Greece to Ukrainian folklore and Modernist literature, to the mobile camera of contemporary cinematography.

A montage tracks Ivanko and Marichka's love as they grow older, both children's physical appearance remaining distinct from the Hutsuls around them, with their simpler clothing and lighter hair colour arranged in a more contemporary style. The montage ends with a close-up of Ivanko in church as a young adult, now played by the iconic

Ivan Mykolaichuk, whose presence in the film became the subject of much puffery in the extensive promotional materials about *Shadows*. Oleksandr Syzonenko's press release for the film states, '[Mykolaichuk] does not perform, but lives in this image' (TsDAMLMU, 607/1/1581: 21). Church bells bridge this gap in years. This close-up matches the look of the young Ivanko, his eyes looking curiously upward in an angelic pose. Whereas Ivanko's close-ups reveal a diegetic origin outside the frame in emulation of medieval iconography, close-ups of Hutsul extras stare directly into the camera for the audience to examine, like Fedir Manailo's Symbolist portraits of Carpathian highlanders. The film cuts to a close-up of Marichka on the balcony of the church, holding a palm leaf and singing with the other women for the beginning of Holy Week. Here, as elsewhere in the story of Ivanko and Marichka, the editing is done in a classical manner to tell a traditional love story. Perhaps the only difference is the lack of an establishing shot in this scene. Marichka slowly walks behind the other women as the camera tracks to the right and pulls out. She descends to the main altar to offer the palm and a candle. She kneels down and Ivanko moves forward. For the first time in the film, we hear non-diegetic symphonic music, which coincides with the classical narrative development in this scene, but this soon fades out to the sound of church bells once again. Paradjanov is gradually normalizing this space with familiar imagery. For Soviet viewers, however, such an uncritical representation of Holy Week celebrations would have been unusual and unexpected. After all, the traditional symbols and contexts of religion in Soviet cinema are entirely absent in *Shadows*: neither the drunken conniving priest, nor the sinister cult-worshiping fanatics make any appearance in the film. Instead, Christian ritual becomes part of everyday life and the ethnic texture of Hutsulshchyna.

The film cuts to a wooden bell tower. The camera pans down to a close-up exterior profile of Marichka, then moves left to a close-up of Ivanko, then right again to Marichka, who begins to walk right, following the camera. A fade follows to a close-up of the two lovers kissing. Blurred tree branches obstruct our view of the action, giving the impression of peering in on an illicit affair. The camera circles around them in close-up as they discuss their love for each other. We briefly emerge within the 'Romeo and Juliet' drama, as Marichka expresses her concern that their families will not let them marry. Non-diegetic symphonic music plays during the entire circular shot. Unfocused branches in the foreground partially obstruct an extreme close-up of Ivanko's hand feeding Marichka berries as she kneels before him. The image blurs as she lies down on her back and the camera moves down her body. The scene stands out in *Shadows* for its atypical lyricism, reminiscent of 1950s Thaw films like Kalatozov's *The Cranes are Flying*. Unlike the spinning camera that follows a traumatic death like that of Oleksa's – which was an original mark of Illienko's authorship in *Shadows* – the circular two-shot resembles the opening scene at the dock with Veronika and Boris. Here, however, Paradjanov implies with this sequence of shots, along with the symbolism of the red berries, the sexual consummation of their relationship, which we soon learn results in Marichka's pregnancy.

The next scene mixes the ethnographic with the development of the lyrical love story. The film cuts to a medium shot of a line of Hutsuls dancing to a diegetic instrumental. The camera tracks across the line of dancers slowly, with the occasional jerk and blur of movement, and then back to the same tracking shot. First the camera moves left and then right. With each blur of movement, the camera cuts to a slightly closer shot, finally stopping on a two-shot of Ivanko and Marichka looking at each other while dancing. They grab each other and start circling, clearly differentiated from the group around them once again, who continue to dance in a line. Marichka moves toward the camera, away from Ivanko, as we see another blur cut, and then a jump to a medium shot as Marichka falls to the ground, foreshadowing her pregnancy. Ivanko moves to help her, eventually dragging her toward the camera. The dance and music continue as the film cuts away to a close-up of a drummer eating corn on the cob.[15] The action parallels many of the earlier scenes of the film, beginning with an ethnographic spectacle involving a group of non-professionals and extras performing as if for the camera, and ending as Ivanko emerges from the group along with the proverbial fourth wall. Thus, the authentic Hutsul folkways meld seamlessly into the artifice of the plot. The concluding shot, however, provides one among many moments of incongruous excess within the film, much like the twins in the church.

Stylistically and narratively, the next scene continues from two scenes prior, while the previous event remains undeveloped and unexplained. A cut takes us to a night scene with wooden structures in silhouette, forming a diagonal criss-cross pattern in the foreground. In a low-angle medium shot, Marichka and Ivanko (the latter also in silhouette) enter the frame from the left. The classic reverse shot structure continues the 'Romeo and Juliet' story, but it remains underdeveloped as a plot, as we see no evidence of the families' continued animosity toward each other. Her growing melancholy appears unmotivated, and we continue to see only glimpses of their relationship before the film cuts to something else. The obstructed foreground and indirect shot angles maintain the sense that we are eavesdropping on these fragments of their socially transgressive love affair.

The next scene, however, alludes to the conflict between the Paliichuks and Hutentiuks as a way to drive the plot forward. Set outside the Paliichuk home, Ivanko's mother complains that the Hutentiuks have taken everything their family had. The camera abruptly pans left to a long shot of Ivanko on the roof of a house. We hear a storm brewing as a handheld camera moves toward him. Ivanko climbs down the ladder – a metaphor for defeated ideals here and elsewhere in *Shadows* – and he and his mother move it to the other side of the house. The handheld camera follows them in a single shot as the two discuss his imminent departure for the mountain to take work as a shepherd. Ivanko leaves the frame and we are left with a high-angle close-up of his mother, mourning her own loneliness. She prays for the souls of her dead children: 'Mykhailo, Danylo, Annychka, Vasyl',[16] Mykola, and Oleksa'. She turns away from the camera and walks into her courtyard, the camera following her. We linger on her as she broodingly recites several lines from the Lord's Prayer. Oleksandr Syzonenko's press release argues that the scene provides further evidence of the film's social consciousness, as it shows how the predatory actions of the *wealthy* Hutentiuks have forced Ivanko to take up wage labour away from their previously self-sufficient family farm (TsDAMLMU, 670/1/1581: 20). Hardly developed in the plot, such an interpretation allowed Dovzhenko Studios to answer Goskino's concerns about the film's apolitical message.

The film cuts to an overhead crane shot of Ivanko walking across a footbridge over the Cheremosh. He exchanges pleasantries with some women washing clothes on the riverbank. Marichka follows, but only after Ivanko leaves from the bottom of the frame. She is touching her belly, providing further clues about her pregnancy. Noticing, the women laugh at her, and ask her if she is sleeping well. The camera moves down to a low-angle close-up of Marichka at the end of the bridge, as she looks back and forth. The only other shot arranged in this manner is at the very beginning of the film, when a high overhead shot looks down on the dead Oleksa. In both cases, it appears that a force of nature is observing these key movements of the plot.

The next scene is an interesting montage that continues the lyric love story, but introduces vague elements of a supernatural influence on the couple's fate. A cut introduces a forested scene as Marichka enters from the right. A *floiar* plays in the background as the camera pans left and Ivanko and Marichka call to each other. In a cutaway we see a deer, which returns throughout the film as a substitute for Marichka after she dies, frequently grazing on her grave. A Hutsul chorus sings a call and response in voice-over as if between Marichka and Ivanko, which ends with a premonition of Ivanko's demise:

On the other side near the stream
Straw was burning.
Come, come to me, my young fellow,
I feel ache without you.

What kind of ache do you feel,
Maybe, this is a headache?
Come, come to me, young fellow,
At least for an hour.

Oh, have a good night, my sweetheart,
Sleep tight up to the morning,
As I go to the mountain pasture
To take a sheep tent.

And I go to the mountain pasture
At that old stable,
And how will I spend the summer,
I wonder, I wonder.
I wonder how to spend the summer,
How will I pasture my sheep?
Oh, I will have to perish
Without you, my Marichka.

In between the verses they struggle to say goodbye. The camera pans slightly left as Ivanko enters the frame. As the couple frolics in the forest clearing, the camera once again circles them in a tight close-up as they bid each other farewell until the winter. Rain begins to come down. She promises to gaze at the star above and think of him while he is gone. The camera stops and backs away from the two. Ivanko moves away, up the mountain, as Marichka moves toward us and to the left. She grabs her head in sorrow. Rain pours down on her, and the camera circles her briefly before cutting to an extreme close-up that follows her pacing back and forth. The Hutsul chorus continues and Ivanko continues up the mountain. Without matching the action, a cut takes the viewer to Marichka, also in long shot, as she walks toward the camera, holding her belly. An old woman in black, probably a witch, walks toward her, cackling that Marichka is getting plump. She offers Marichka blueberries – a fruit with both medicinal qualities and dark magic in Carpathian folklore (they also contrast with the sexual connotations of the red berries that Ivanko feeds her earlier in the chapter) – and touches her belly: 'What have you got there?' the woman asks as Marichka runs away. The scene fades to red again as the old woman laughs and Marichka holds her face in shame.

While maintaining the eclectic style of the first part of the movie, the 'Ivanko and Marichka' chapter remains the clearest example of classical narrative development within the film. Here, we have a traditional story of a pair of young lovers forced apart because the man has to get a job to support his widowed mother. The woman, meanwhile, struggles with the stigma of an unexpected pregnancy outside of wedlock. Most of the camera work in this chapter comes directly from Illienko, and contains little of the static tableaux that Paradjanov favoured. The camera places the audience in the uneasy position as clandestine spectators to the love story throughout most of chapter, even as the more classical techniques employed in the forest scene make it one of the most satisfying and beautiful sequences in the film.

'THE MOUNTAIN PASTURE'

The title of the second chapter – *Polonyna* in Ukrainian – refers to the uniquely unforested Carpathian highlands used for sheep and goat pastures during the summer and autumn. Almost devoid of a comprehensible narrative, the chapter also denies the audience an intertitled explanation. The chapter begins with the sound of a man's echoed call, and then a *floiar* plays to a montage of moss on rocks, suggesting the impressionistic natural abstractions in Ogata Korin's paintings. A cut to a low-angle long shot introduces Myko, Ivanko's best friend and a mute (played by the famous Russian-Armenian clown and mime Leonid Engibarov), with sticks on his back, climbing to the top of the mountain pasture as the echoed singing continues. We return to a montage, this time of tree bark in extreme close-up, and then back to a medium shot of Myko. A montage of mud, grass and water follows, and then back to a medium shot of the mute. He lays down the sticks, coughs and collapses on the ground without explanation. The film's characters constantly have extreme reactions to inexplicable stimuli, in a surrealistic take on melodramatic conventions. Moreover, Paradjanov clearly had more creative control over the first part of this chapter with its surrealistic juxtapositions and static framing.

A cut takes us to a high-angle long shot of three *trembitary* raising their instruments as the echoed chant fades with the blare of their *trembity*. Finally, we see Ivanko in close-up, with cow parsnip flowers in his hat to ward off mosquitoes and a satisfied smile on his face. The *trembity* are still playing off-camera as the film cuts to an extreme long shot of men herding sheep. The beautiful bird's-eye view reveals a herd of flawlessly white sheep filling a circular closing the colour of black earth. The horizon is tilted with a small wooden dwelling in the background and even higher mountains in the distance. The shot resembles a traditional mountain vista with its extreme depth at the top of the frame, while flattening the space of the bottom and rendering it as a two-dimensional canvas. In a low angle close-up, the weathered and moustachioed head shepherd [*vatah*] played by seasoned Ukrainian actor Mykola Hryn'ko, who also appeared in most of Tarkovsky's films, offers viewers an explanation of how to herd sheep, in many ways bound into the film's spectacle of Hutsul folkways and material culture. In a brief moment of narrative development, Ivanko takes off his hat and introduces himself to the shepherd, asking for a job. We return to another long shot from above of five men kneeling to pray in the upper third of the frame, while a herd of sheep fill the bottom two-thirds. As in the shot described above, the long lens flattens the perspective in an illusion of a two-dimensional canvas. As with the earlier shot, this one too lasts several seconds. We should not confuse these two high overhead shots with the two described earlier in the film. Whereas the earlier shots, which include Oleksa under the tree and Ivanko and Marichka crossing the river, derive from an unspecified point of view, these shots of the mountain pasture are objective, immobile and contemplative in their length. The aesthetic of these latter shots derive from painting rather than the cinema.

The next scene, which is ethnographic in orientation, explores rituals of food preparation among the shepherds. The film cuts to an interior shot of men chopping wood for the fire, and then to an extreme close-up of hands husking corn to the sound of a strong wind outside. We return to the interior medium shot. The shepherds huddle around a fire as Myko enters with his sticks. The men dry their clothes over the fire as rain leaks through the roof. In close-up, hands reach into a pail of milk. After several moments, a lump of *brynza*[17] cheese emerges as the *vatah* tells a mythical story about the birth of the Carpathians. The mute attempts to act out the story for Ivanko, the latter as usual a

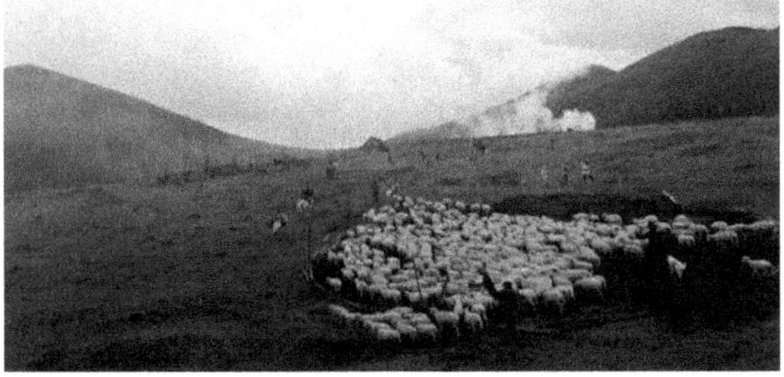

Figure 8: The highland pasture.
Still from the film.

stand-in for the viewer. Eventually, he walks out of the tent, because the shepherd's story reminds him of his fraught relationship with Marichka.

The action sequence that follows is a confusing montage of hallucinations and divine omens, and ends with Marichka's accidental death and Ivanko's discovery of her body washed away by the Cheremosh. The scene begins as an exterior long shot. Ivanko lies down near the sheep to sleep, but a shot reverse shot reveals his discovery of a twinkling star in the evening sky. He drifts off to sleep and we consequently understand the subsequent scene to be his dream, when in fact the consequences are real. An extreme close-up of Marichka is framed on a bed of hay, which alongside the guiding light of the twinkling star functions as a biblical reference to the manger in Bethlehem. She also sees the twinkling star, indicated with a similar shot reverse shot. Marichka gets up while looking toward the star. The camera tilts upward and follows her as a *floiar* plays. A cut follows and we see a mountainside as sheep descend, having escaped their closing in the mountain pasture. The camera is moving about, emulating the confusing series of events: men fire their rifles; Marichka walks through the forest, seemingly following the twinkling star. The camera is now in front of her, moves up to her and rests on a close-up as she stops. Finally, Ivanko emerges from his slumber, which further confounds our understanding of the events. Mist obstructs the action. A *trembita* blares and we hear men calling out. A cut takes us to Marichka, still walking through the forest to follow the star. Eventually, she breaks into a run, a handheld camera following her, interjected with several blurred jump cuts. The film then suddenly cuts to a sheep that falls off a cliff, and then to a high angle long shot of three *trembitary* who blare their horns. The film then returns to a medium shot of Marichka on an extremely narrow outcropping of a cliff face, trying to rescue a ram that is stranded there. Suspenseful music plays as she closes in on the animal. She grabs hold of the ram as the film cuts to a close-up of it in her arms. Joyfully, she calls to Ivanko, but a close-up of her foot reveals that she has lost her balance, suggesting again nature's cruelty in the film. The ram drowns in the Cheremosh and is swept downstream, before we see a cutaway to the star. In a visual citation of the woman in black with the baby carriage from Sergei Eisenstein's *Bronenosets Potemkin / Battleship Potemkin* (1925), we see a close-up of Marichka gradually falling. In both shots, we see an image of a beautiful death, analogous to an image of the Crucifixion or another early Christian martyrdom. Moreover, in both *Battleship Potemkin* and *Shadows*, the women die after attempting to save the innocents – a baby and a lamb, respectively – which is a fitting conclusion to a sequence ripe with Christian symbolism.

Marichka appears in the water, struggling against the current. She falls before the cut to a close-up of three men, the middle one calling out for help with an archetypical Hutsul chant. Far different from the painterly and ethnographic beginning of the chapter, this scene evokes a children's fairy tale, with its association of dreams with reality, and

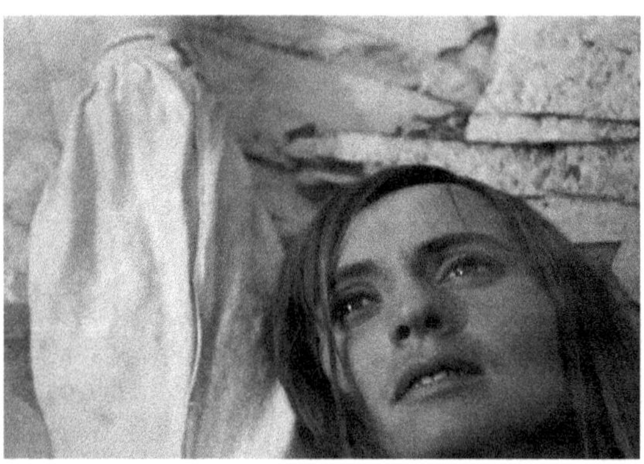

Figure 9: Marichka falls to her death. Still from the film.

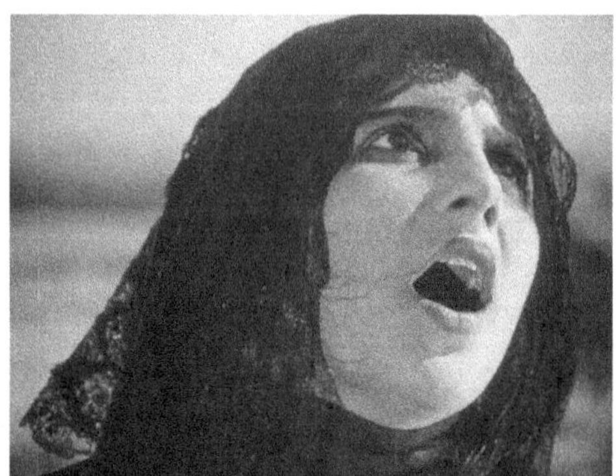

Figure 10: Woman in black falls to her death. Still from *Battleship Potemkin* (Eisenstein, 1925).

natural processes with the mystical powers of the heavens. The star itself is a common symbol of an unattainable ideal. In Marichka's case, she hopes to rescue the lost livestock, a perpetual symbol of childhood and innocence; in Ivanko's situation, he follows the star to Marichka to rekindle their love before he left for the highland pasture.

We abruptly return to an ethnographic view of a hunting party carrying a dead bear on a stick. The air is filled with the smoke of torches that light the dawn. As in later scenes, smoke generally signals death, but it also identifies a point of contact between the heavens and earth. A jerky moving camera surveys a village scene of men with torches searching the woods and riverbank. And then to tragedy: Ivanko appears in the shot suddenly, much as he does in earlier shots. He greets a group of Hutsuls in the traditional manner – 'Praise Jesus!' ['*Slava Iesu!*'] – but they only stare at him in response. Eventually, a confused Ivanko approaches Myko to ask him what has happened. After he fails to understand, Ivanko returns to the river. Women on the riverbank are already lamenting Marichka. A jerky camera follows Ivanko in close-up. Marichka's mother asks her husband to find their daughter. The film cuts to a POV shot, apparently from Ivanko, until he appears in the shot with a torch. He approaches the camera, having become aware of what has happened. Floating down the Cheremosh on a log raft led by a *bokorash*,[18] Ivanko is splayed out on top like his brother Oleksa at the beginning of the film. We move in to a close-up of Ivanko, still on the raft, as a *floiar* plays. The camera moves in its characteristic arch when revealing a dead body, starting from Ivanko's face in close-up, up to the sky, and then down to a long shot of women surrounding Marichka, who is now wrapped in linen (just as Joseph of Arimathea does with the body of Christ). The camera jerks back to Ivanko and then returns to Marichka. The camera moves toward her, beginning as Ivanko's point of view until he enters the frame from the bottom. We see him from above, walking through the water, and the camera follows. Women chant as Ivanko emerges from the water toward the body. The camera circles around and arcs to Marichka's body again. Finally, we return to a wide shot of Ivanko and the body on the very edge of the frame. Most of the frame encompasses a sandy beach, rocks and driftwood. The shot lasts several seconds, as chanting fades out and fast-paced symphonic music gets louder and louder. After several static moments, a handheld camera jerkily darts toward Ivanko, resting on a blurry close-up as he realizes that she is dead. The camera remains on Ivanko's terror-stricken face for several seconds, and then moves left to reveal Marichka's feet on the edge of the frame. The film fades to red. As Efird (2014: 28) writes: 'This elaborate long take forms a composite of subject and object, albeit one in a seemingly perpetual state of fluctuation'. The scene, however, is merely an extreme form of Illienko's blending of subjective and objective perspective common throughout *Shadows*. In the end, however, Ivanko emerges as the object of the gaze, rather than its subject, suggesting his new vulnerability after Marichka's death. For the first time, for example, we see the protagonist in a high-angle shot.

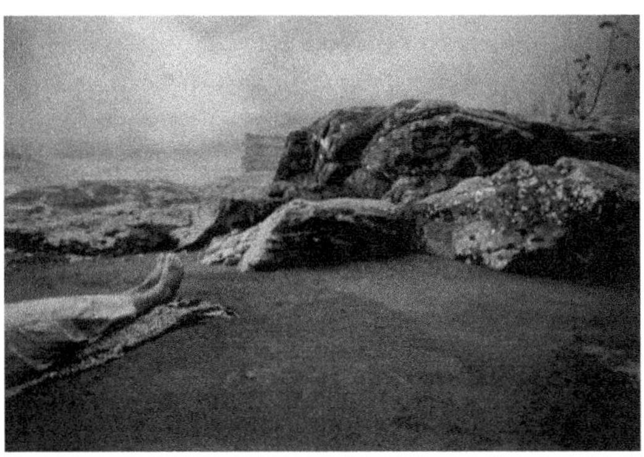

Figure 11: Ivanko discovers Marichka's body washed ashore. Still from the film.

Similar to the two earlier burials, Ivanko plants a birch cross for Marichka on top of a hill. Unlike Oleksa's and Petro's funerals, however, this one is unaccompanied by a procession or *trembity*. Ivanko is very much alone, despite the girl's parents being alive. The camera follows him left, looking up from the bottom of the hill as he walks toward us. The camera continues to move toward the left as he falls on a log in grief. He gets up, struggles forward, and the camera once again spins in an arcing motion up to the sky and around to the cross on the hill. Again, we seem to have entered Ivanko's point of view as we move back to where we came from. The camera scales the hill and moves toward the deer sitting next to the grave as a *floiar* plays. And then, while the camera looks up, still seemingly in Ivanko's point of view, he emerges from the right side of the frame, walking toward the deer (now seemingly in possession of Marichka's soul, in an opaque re-enactment of a paganistic Resurrection) in the centre of the frame, with arms outstretched. The deer runs off to the right, and we are left with a medium shot of Ivanko and the cross in the frame. Once again, the film fades to red to signify the end of the chapter. The death of Marichka thus exists within an entirely symbolic universe, alternately pagan and Christian, and motivated only by machinations of an abstract fate.

'LONELINESS'

The beginning of the next chapter returns us to the archaic convention of the intertitle: 'People considered that he was lost to his great affliction, and girls composed little songs about their love…' The intertitle is directly from Kotsiubyns'kyi, but Paradjanov diverges from the novella by filling in the story of a lost Ivanko, rather than simply losing him for six years 'on the Hungarian side' of the mountains (Kotsiubyns'kyi 1967: 49). Here, the narrative of Ivanko and Marichka has entered a folkloric space, and the chapter's soundscape is littered with the rumours that will constitute their mythology.

We begin with an interior shot in silhouette, looking out to a hearth fire in the foreground. An open door in the background allows us to see a herd of sheep and the shepherds in the background. One of the men asks Ivanko to come to his wedding, while the wind swings the door open and shut. Ivanko stands on the threshold of the darkened interior as the camera remains on the flapping door for several moments. A fade is followed by a high-angle exterior shot of the Paliichuk courtyard. From our view on to the roof of the house, we see Ivanko and his mother prepare for a journey. An off-camera conversation between two women offers exposition of Ivanko's life in the intervening years, and further solidifies Ivanko's new relationship with the viewer as an object of the gaze: 'What a fine lad he was, but now he's unhappy, unkempt, in tattered clothes, and dirty, like a poor, old man'. If at first we perceive the world of the Hutsuls through Ivanko's eyes, we now look upon the protagonist mediated through the gossip of local women. Ivanko has let himself and his home go to ruin after Marichka died. From the roof, we follow him through the courtyard. After he exits the yard through the gate, the camera tracks down to the ground, and we see Ivanko's haggard and unkempt appearance. The women tell us that he has sold all his sheep to a rich man. The dishevelled Ivanko, with a bag tied to his axe, sets off toward the camera, as the gossiping women, now seen in the background, whisper more quietly. A fade leads to a high-angle medium shot of Ivanko in winter, eating on top of a dirt mound. The camera pans up and we realize that he is at a cemetery, digging a grave. Another off-camera conversation – this time between two men – reveals that Ivanko has been digging the same hole for five years. The camera tracks upward to a long shot of the graveyard. The men continue to discuss what a shame it is that love did this to him. Another fade takes us to a medium shot of Ivanko kneeling in the river washing his clothes, as we hear another woman lamenting off-camera that there is no one to wash his clothes and cook for him. The film cuts to an exterior close-up of Ivanko on the left edge of the frame. He leans against a newly constructed house, playing a *drymba*, as a woman explains that their old house collapsed and they had to sell their last cow. She reveals (to us?) that she hired Ivanko to build the new house, but he never works. The camera moves out to reveal only a half-finished façade with an axe stuck on the top of a door frame against the background of a woman, a child and the evening sky. Such 'visual jokes', as Nebesio (1994: 45) calls such movements of the camera, constitute one

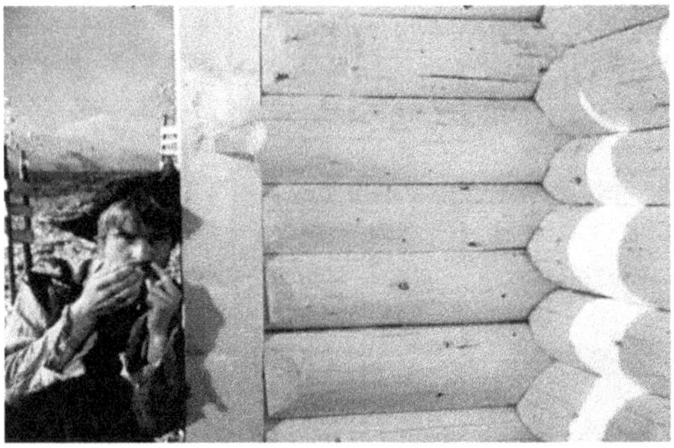

Figure 12: Ivanko in decline. Still from the film.

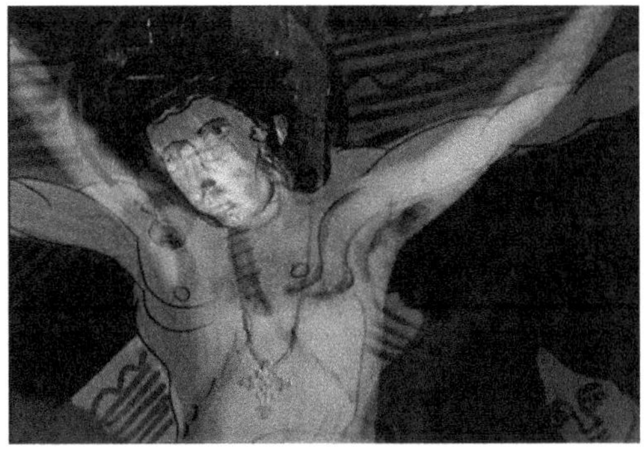

Figure 13: Myko superimposed on the crucifix. Still from the film.

among many direct interactions between the film-makers and the audience. The film fades to a low-angle shot of a church as Ivanko climbs down a ladder from the roof. The long shot follows him, tilting down as women continue to gossip off-screen about his tattered clothes and reclusive attitude. The camera pans left with him as he seeks warmth in a rock-enclosed shrine next to the church, with only candles to warm his frozen hands. Ivanko has now been hired to fix the steeple, but approaches the task in a similar attitude of depressed inattention. We hear the sound of a strong wind as the film fades to a close-up of the now extinguished candles. The entire sequence of Ivanko's decline is brought together via the sound of off-screen gossip and a bleak grey tonality using black-and-white film stock (apart from the final transitional shot of the candles, which is in vivid colour) – a style that will be replicated in later works of poetic cinema, such as Illienko's own directorial debut, *Krynytsia dlia sprahlykh*/*A Well for the Thirsty* (1965) and Leonid Osyka's masterpiece *Kaminnyi khrest*/*The Stone Cross* (1967). According to Ol'ha Briukhovets'ka (2002: 30), the narrative structure is also radically different in this chapter from the rest of the film: 'In "Loneliness" the narrative's cyclical mode is completely torn', and yet the film does not emerge within a linear mode. Rather, the vignettes of Ivanko simultaneously present his decline while offering a static, 'synchronous' image of his state of being after Marichka's death.

The film fades to an interior shot of a crucifix with a barely recognizable drawing behind it on the wooden cross, bleeding over onto the boards of the church wall and mimicking Christ's pose. Ivanko's friend Myko is superimposed onto the drawing in the style of Paradjanov's own works of collage art that mix the imagery of religious icons, Renaissance art and cartoonish surrealism. Next, a drawing of a woman's face and arm is superimposed onto a close-up of Ivanko, first as a boy and then as a man, both looking curiously but frightfully off-screen. The adult Ivanko is now dressed well and clean-shaven, but still warming his hands with his breath. A fade brings us to another superimposed image, this time of Paradjanov's drawing of hands with Myko's face. The mute reveals bloodied hands and carries a crown of vines that, after another fade, catch fire. Other hands become visible through the superimposed drawings being warmed over the burning crown. Finally, a lamb with three sets of hands on it is superimposed onto a fresco of the Old Testament Trinity. The film fades finally to the same fresco with three identically dressed moustachioed *drymba* players in the foreground. They wear *kresani* and rough *serdaky*, and look directly into the camera as they play their instruments in unison. The entire sequence appears overdetermined by its metaphoric associations, but Paradjanov refuses to connect them in any meaningful or obvious way to the plot.

The film returns us to the grey exterior landscape of the previous sequence. A half-frozen Ivanko is tending sheep near the church, as we hear the cries of a child announcing Christmas morning. Ivanko grabs a young goat while the camera follows him to the left, singing and dancing along with the boy's words that 'Christ is born!' The camera jerks to the left, focusing on a snow-covered scene with one fir tree and two small figures in long shot at its base. Off-screen, women chatter about drinking with Magyars on Christmas Eve, as the camera jerks back to a close-up of Ivanko and the goat. They giggle about giving Ivanko some vodka. The camera jerks left again to reveal Myko carrying a small fir and a gun, which he fires into the air before collapsing. Once again, Myko's presence is entirely allegorical: he attempts to act but is foiled by his own cruel nature. As the women talk about Ivanko's drunken antics, a line of drunken carollers follow him. The camera follows the group to the right as they enter Ivanko's manger, offering him more vodka as they enter. A cut takes us to an extreme low-angle shot of Ivanko climbing a leafless tree as the camera circles from its base, following the man to the top, and eventually stopping as he grabs the last apple, which functions as another turning point in the plot. While the use of the circling camera signals another love for Ivanko, the apple suggests that it will be one of more earthly concerns.

The film now cuts to a flood of spring colour – orange, brown and pale green – as the film moves left, following a well-dressed Ivanko and his mother on horseback, with blurred foliage in the foreground. A band follows them as we hear the sounds of a chorus chanting a song that equates marriage with abduction, and the consummation of that relationship sadly equated with a blossoming apple tree:

Oh, behind branches there is a moon,
Behind branches,
Oh, there is only you, young girl,
Just outside the village [*zasillia*].
Oh, they saddled grey horses,
They saddled,
And prepared the young girl for marriage,
They abducted [*zbyraly*] her.

Oh, bow down, young girl,
Down to the earth,
As your bitter fate is
Nearby.
Oh, an apple tree bloomed
With white blossom,
The young girl began crying
Bitterly.

The camera jerks back and forth, blurring the colours once again like an impressionist painting. From the position of a densely forested spot, the camera spins around to the sound of music playing and Hutsuls dancing outside in a circular clearing. The camera continues to spin amidst the revellers, occasionally pausing on an individual, a berry on a tree, a couple dancing, a pistol; all in close-up, but obscured by the out-of-focus foliage.

Finally, the film cuts to a fire set against the black background of a forge as the chorus continues. Another trick image, the camera quickly moves out to reveal a young woman lifting her skirt up to reveal her calf, and her foot tapping the ground in a fluid motion. As the camera continues to move back, we see that she is stepping on a bellows to feed the fire. The camera pans right to reveal Ivanko and a white horse in the courtyard. The woman re-enters the frame from the left, walks over to Ivanko and kisses him. As a jerky camera ascends to a high-angle shot of the couple, together they shoe the horse. A close-up of the woman, Palahna (played by Tat'iana Bestaeva, and imparting on the character a beauty and complexity utterly lacking in Kotsiubyns'kyi's more misogynistic understanding of her role in the plot), reveals her printed floral headscarf and lots of jewellery around her neck. As she looks down

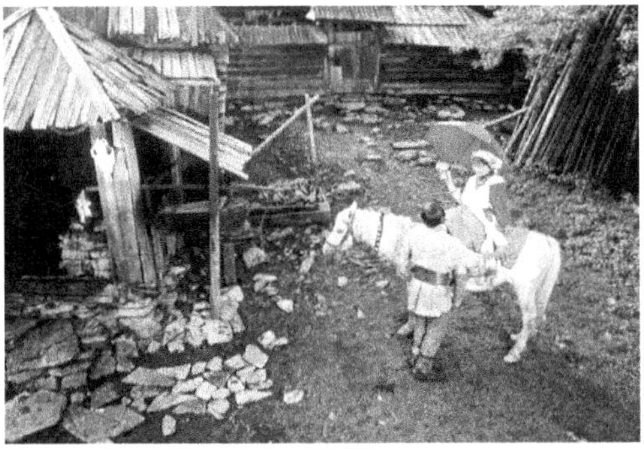

Figure 14: Palahna on the horse, with red umbrella. Still from the film.

suggestively at the off-screen Ivanko, we notice her oiled and styled hair and liberally-applied make-up. Also an outsider, Palahna's appearance indicates her connection to the marketplace of mass-produced commodities, which is in sharp contrast to the handicraft production elsewhere in the film's ethnoscape. Consequently, Paradjanov compels us to interrogate her authenticity. We see a close-up of the horse's hoof as the couple hammers the shoe in, and then a high-angle close-up of Ivanko from Palahna's point of view. With three nails in his mouth, he looks up at her and smiles suggestively, and then the camera moves back to its previous spot above the courtyard. Palahna sits aside the horse, once again with her calves conspicuously revealed; Ivanko hands her an anachronistically modern red umbrella, which she flirtatiously lets fall to the other side of the horse as she herself falls into Ivanko's arms. As is true with much of *Shadows of Forgotten Ancestors*, the scene breaks the action into delineated moments of interaction, removing the build-up and consequences in the process. More significant for understanding Paradjanov's own developing tableaux aesthetic, the previous image of Palahna on the horse evokes a painterly canvas of surreal juxtapositions; not only between the ethnographic depiction of Hutsulshchyna and the world of commodity culture, but also between Victorian notions of feminine virtue with the use of the side-saddle pose and Palahna's unequivocal sexuality.

The film cuts to the leafless tree from the beginning of the sequence as the camera continues to circle around it slowly. Ivanko emerges from the bottom of the frame with the apple that he has picked. As he takes a bite in close-up, his eyes stare into the sky absent-mindedly; an indication that he has reacquired his youthful curiosity. The apple at once signifies his return to the world of the living, and the beginning of his life squarely in the material world cut off from his ideal (Marichka), the latter of which ultimately leads to his death. An intertitle tells us that 'Ivan' gets married, but now has to 'manage the household [*hazduvaty*]', something his mother has neglected since the deaths of Oleksa and Petro (as exposed by one of the off-camera women, Evdokiia, at the beginning of the chapter 'Loneliness'). We then fade to red as the next chapter begins.

'IVAN AND PALAHNA'

The chapter opens with a low-angle interior shot of a large one-room structure, as three old women bathe Ivanko in a barrel and another spins yarn on the right. In voice-over, one of the women reveals that his mother is now dead, before two of them dry him with a white cloth with embroidered designs. The film cuts to a young fir tree, a symbol of spring, fertility and immortality; the camera then abruptly moves back and then up with a lurch to reveal an old woman with an axe, who chops it down and holds it unceremoniously by its thin trunk. Such an inexplicable action, rendered as both shocking and violent with the jerky movement of the camera, suggests an ominous tone to what should be a joyous occasion. The film returns to the entrance of the courtyard as another wedding chorus begins, this time imagining a bride waiting for her beloved to bring her new clothes for the wedding:

> There is a willow
> There is a willow plank, plank,
> Nastechka, Nastechka
> Nastechka, Nastechka walks on it.
> She looks, looks around
> She looks, looks around the whole field
> Searching for her beloved
> Searching for her beloved to come.
> Where from he
> Where from he should come.
> What he will bring
> What he will bring for Nastechka.
> He will bring red high boots,
> He will bring red high boots, high boots.
> Made in Kosov,
> Made in Kosov, in Kosov.
> He's coming!
> [...] Cast mercy on the one
> who loved me and gave his life,
> cast mercy.
> [...] Rein for the sake of truth
> and beauty, and holy truth...
> [...] And they were worn
> And they were worn in Kryvorivnia.

While certainly more upbeat than the first wedding dirge, it nonetheless interprets marriage through the language of the market and exchange value rather than love. Moreover, the willow carries very different connotations than the fir, and is understood as the tree of wish fulfilment.

A finely-dressed Ivanko appears from the structure to the right, with black and white rooster feathers stuck in his hat, suggesting his pride before the wedding. He bows to a group of old women and moves toward the camera, pausing at the entrance in a low-angle medium shot. He exits the frame to the right as women in black, one with a wreath made from the felled fir tree, follow him. The camera follows them around the house to the back entrance, but stops as a dove emerges from the doorway and lands on the wreath in the woman's hands, mixing symbols in a puzzling manner. Ivanko and the women bow to each other awkwardly and he sets off by himself to the right. The women cross themselves several times and the scene cuts. The mash-up of symbolic references in the opening of the scene deliberately seeks to confuse the audience, or perhaps suggests complex and contradictory emotions that Ivanko was experiencing before his marriage to the wealthy, beautiful but vulgar and empty Palahna.

An extreme high-angle long shot shows Ivanko on a lake, rowing a primitive log raft diagonally across the darkened frame, ominously evoking the scene where he discovers Marichka's body on the Cheremosh. The brief shot is striking in its divergence from the colour scheme of the rest of the chapter. Grigorian (2011: 106) likens the shot to the crossing of the River Styx into the underworld of an unsatisfying marriage. The film cuts to an extreme low-angle shot of a girl on a rooftop shouting: 'He's coming!' The handheld camera moves back, tilting down in a self-conscious move to catch a close-up of Ivanko as he walks across the frame from left to right. We follow him as he turns around suspiciously (at us?) and then continues walking to the right. The camera stops and, as he leaves the frame to the right, shoots up and over a house to reveal a courtyard in a long shot, with two men sitting next to a cow on the far side. Ivanko enters and looks curiously at the camera positioned on the rooftop. He walks to the centre of the stone courtyard and bows again. Four women emerge from the right side of the frame and bow to Ivanko, after which they escort him into the structure to the right. This and the next shots required elaborate choreography and, as James Steffen (2013: 70) writes, 'illustrates the extent to which [Paradjanov] has consolidated his skills as a director', thus contradicting Illienko's (2008b: 83) claim that he merely 'placed objects in front of the camera'. If we are to believe Luhovs'kyi, however, this may have been a scene for which Paradjanov was absent, and thus directed by Illienko. After all, the mobile cinematic style that uncovers an increasingly complex set within a single shot reveals the clear influence of Urusevskii, even as the associational elements of the felled fir and the dove evoke Paradjanov's aesthetic of the uncanny. This latter aesthetic is most pronounced in the next scene, perhaps the most famous one in the film.

The film cuts to an interior still life of two scarves against a black background in the left two-thirds of the screen, while the right third reveals an aisle with a striped rug and man standing in a doorway in the background. He bows and lets Ivanko inside, the latter ducking to get through. This is a frequent motif: doorways are never high enough for him. He stops and bows to the camera as the black background opens downward to reveal another trick image: an open-topped chest behind which sits a row of young women on the left side of the room and an older woman in the foreground. Ivanko looks at them and bows again as one of them rises to place a ceremonial cloth [*rushnyk*] around his eyes as a blindfold. Two women then lead him to the chest in the foreground, where he sits with his back to the camera. Two men in white shirts and black trousers enter the room with a yoke. After they bow, the film jumps to a reverse shot that reveals a circle of women behind Ivanko. The one closest to Ivanko spins around, and we see that Palahna too is blindfolded and escorted to the chest upon which Ivanko is still sitting. The men enter the frame and place the yoke around both of their heads before the frame empties of everyone except them. The film cuts to a two shot of the enyoked couple, with icons and candles burning behind them. The yoke was Paradjanov's invention, although he claimed that Hutsul songs about the proverbial 'yoke' of marriage (see the song above for an example) suggested use of the device in the scene. Moreover, he claimed, the Hutsul extras agreed that it was a nice touch (Paradzhanov 1966: 63).

Ivanko frees himself of the yoke as Palahna smiles. The film cuts to a close-up of the yoke on the end and bottom of Palahna's exquisitely patterned red, orange and yellow dress, socks and black sandals. The yoke is thrown aside as Ivanko's feet enter the frame. He walks around her, gradually undressing Palahna, her clothes falling to the floor.

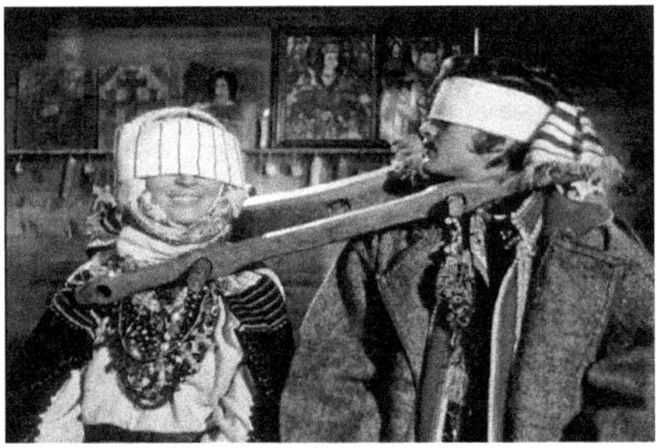

Figure 15: Ivanko and Palahna enyoked. Still from the film.

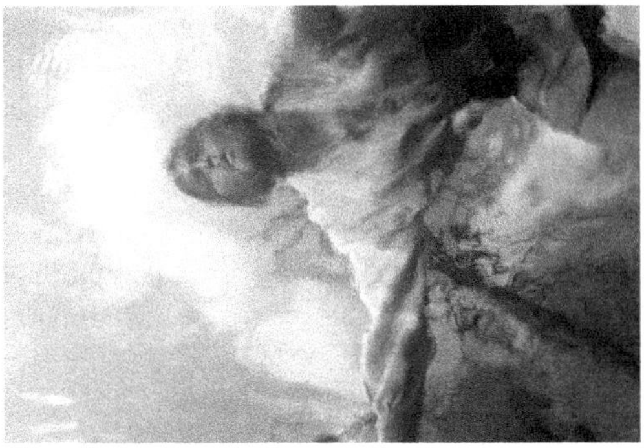

Figure 16: Ivanko from the depths. Still from the film.

Her white linen undergarment is lifted up and her calves are revealed again. A cut takes us to a close-up of the back of Palahna's head, her auburn hair now down for the first time, not unlike Marichka's contemporary urban style. She slowly turns around and, with bare shoulders, looks down to her left and then up, with widened eyes and a heaving chest. Ivanko's still clothed hand reaches into the frame from the right, and rips her sole remaining necklace off to her frightened and then sensual look. A close-up of Ivanko's hand becomes a visual repetition of an earlier close-up during which he fed berries to a kneeling Marichka. This time, he opens his hand to reveal the necklace as he slowly lets its beads fall to the floor. In 1965, such a scene was unquestionably the most explicit sex scene in Soviet cinema. The beads function differently in this respect, however, associating sexuality with death rather than life. Whereas Marichka bears a child, we soon learn that Palahna cannot. As usual, the film fades to red as the next chapter begins.

'ROUTINE'

At less than five minutes in length, the next chapter is the shortest in the film and is also devoid of any dialogue. Paradjanov's shocking sexual innuendo returns in the next scene with an exterior close-up of Ivanko wearing an absurdly phallic wooden holster. He takes out a stone from the holster to sharpen his scythe as the camera cuts to another close-up of that action. A final handheld close-up shows him cutting hay with his scythe. Meanwhile, Palahna stomps on the bail, seemingly dancing around the spool. Finally, the film cuts to a two-shot with Ivanko's now shaven face in the foreground and Palahna behind him, the former loading the hay on the bale. The woman collapses in giggling as Ivanko helps her to the ground. They embrace each other, Palahna with passion but Ivanko with indifference. After he rejects her advances and walks away, Palahna collapses on the ground in disappointment. Clearly, the chapter's provocative opening image suggests Ivanko's sexual frustration, along with his attempts to repress it with routine tasks. For the final shot, the film reveals a low-angle shot taken from underwater, with the now familiar sound of the *drymba*. Ivanko appears at the edge of the frame and bends over, moving toward the camera to take a drink from the pond before the scene fades to red. The costly shot appears radically different in a film that tends to view the action either as a divine presence from above or as a bystander. Here we see the action from the depths, predicting Ivanko's eventual downfall. At the same time, the water distorts the image, transforming it into an exquisite and impressionistic canvas.

'CHRISTMAS'

The chapter opens with sounds of East European bagpipes [*volynky*], as a line of costumed men parade before the camera in a close-up. Although Hutsuls typically dress up for Easter, Paradjanov took artistic licence here by presenting this scene at Christmas (Paradzhanov 1966: 63). We see a parade of ethnicities and animals: a Polish noble, a Hungarian hussar, a bear, a Turk, among others, before the appearance of the Grim Reaper provokes the camera to jerk far to the left to reveal Marichka's birch-tree fashioned grave with the deer grazing in front of it. We slowly move back to the Reaper as he takes off his mask to reveal himself as Ivanko, implying his increasing unhappiness and fixation on death. As the camera hovers on his face for several moments, we see his faint and anxious appearance. The film cuts to a high-angle long shot of festivities inside Ivanko and Palahna's courtyard to the sound of a Hutsul chorus about a starving little goat, whose horns are all that are left of her:

> Oh, good evening to this home!
> Would you allow a mama goat to hop around?
> Would you allow a mama goat to hop around?
> Oh, hop-hop, you goat.

Our lord sowed a lot of wheat.
Our lord sowed a lot of wheat.
Wheat is overgrown on the field,
There is nothing to reap,
There is nothing
to feed her little goat with in winter.
There is nothing
to feed her little goat with in winter.
Oh, I went to a steep mount
To pasture a little goat
for two or three hours.
To pasture a little goat
for two or three hours.
Oh, she went over steep mountains
To get her little goat of three years
Oh, mama went over steep mountains
And did not find her little goat,
but only her horns,
And did not find her little goat,
but only its horns,
One horn she used to brew beer,
The other one she used
to sit her guests.
The other one she used
to sit her guests.
Eat, dear guests, pour wine,
And remember about our little goat.
And remember about our little goat.

The revellers eventually leave as Palahna picks up their trash. Seconds later, a man re-enters the courtyard and seemingly rapes her. As the camera eventually moves to the right, Ivanko is revealed to be looking on from outside the other entrance. The camera surveys a glove and the apple on the snowy ground, and then moves up to a weathered Palahna with another apple in her hand. Here again, the apple's connotation with the fall from paradise suggests an earthly love, one that is violent and vulgar. She looks around as the camera jerkily pans to the courtyard entrance, with Ivanko's scythe noticeable on the right side of the doorframe. She walks outside to meet him, with the camera following in close-up the entire time. Palahna tries to reassure her husband as an old woman appears in their midst wailing about her missing child: 'Ivanko, where is my child? Palahna, where is my child? My child is imprisoned like a criminal'. Her wails begin at the moment that the song of the starving goat ends, further implying a direct parallel between missing or dead livestock and children. The final shot of the scene is a close-up of another costumed man (Palahna's rapist in this case). He removes his mask to reveal a sinister-looking Hutsul with a necklace of dried peppers and corn – the accoutrements of a sorcerer – along with slanted eyebrows, sunken cheeks and a thick moustache. His appearance is not so much atypical of a Hutsul man as it is a parody of him. The presence of the sorcerer also signals a change in the film's symbolic world: whereas the first half of *Shadows* referenced Greco-Roman mythology and the Gospels, the second half views Hutsul everyday life as profoundly animistic.

The film cuts to an exterior low-angle medium shot of the Paliichuk home as Ivanko exits into the courtyard, ducking as he passes through the doorway (as always). He now dresses as a wealthy Hutsul, with a fine kidskin coat adorned with objects to ward off evil spirits. The camera follows him as he feeds the animals, affectionately bleating along with them as if they are his children, before returning to the doorway to kneel and offer an appeal to 'sorcerers and demons'. In the longest piece of spoken dialogue in the entire film, Ivanko calls out: 'Come, sorcerers and demons! Souls of drowned men, come to my feast with rich plates and sweet honey vodka! But I ask: after that, vanish, never to return!' Ivanko has become an anonymous Hutsul, subject to the whims of demons and sorcerers, rather than carving his own path with his love for Marichka. A now patronizing Palahna is heard off-screen calling 'Ivan' (rather than the diminutive forms, 'Iva' or 'Ivanko') to dinner. In a medium shot of the couple, their backs to the camera, they offer prayers in front of a table full of food. Both are dressed as wealthy Hutsuls, with ornate *serdaky*. In a series of close-ups, they ask God to allow 'lost souls' and those 'hurt on long journeys or downed in deep waters' to join them. Ivanko looks expectantly at his wife to complete the prayers before he, and then Palahna, blow over each other's shoulders to ward away the demons. The film cuts back to the dinner table, this time with the couple sitting behind it and facing the camera as they cross themselves. A calf also shares dinner with them. They silently eat and drink next to each other for a few seconds before Ivanko takes a bottle of vodka and a bowl with pancakes [*blinchiki*] and leaves the table. The camera remains on a rejected Palahna for several seconds before cutting to Ivanko as he prepares to eat in the other room. The lonely scene is interrupted by children who barge into their home singing carols. With the calf in hand, he joins the children to sing, much as he had done during the previous Christmas before marrying Palahna. He turns to the camera as it moves toward him and asks Palahna: 'Where are my children? Where are my goats?' He sings the last question several times as he spins around. Palahna covers the uneaten food as we hear Ivanko continue to sing the question: 'Where are my goats?' several times. He enters the frame from the bottom and begins to undress with Palahna's help before climbing hopelessly into his bed as she falls onto the dinner bench.

Ivanko dreams of Marichka as the film begins one of its more beautiful scenes. A cut takes us to a close-up interior of the window with Ivanko's vodka and *blinchiki* sitting uneaten on the ledge, and then to a close-up of the sleeping man. A bell rings and the film cuts to a series of shots of Marichka's face behind the window frame: her lips, chin and neck, and finally back to her whole face, her long hair covering the left half of her face. Her hand touches the bottom-right pane, just behind the now visible bottle of vodka. Then Marichka's face is in the upper-left pane with each hand touching the bottom two, then to a profile, and then to her hand behind the bottle. Marichka's presence on the other side of the window suggests that she and Ivanko exist within different worlds: Ivanko in the earthly world of flesh and money, whereas Marichka in the heavenly world of childhood and love. Grigorian (2011: 109) refers to these two worlds as the 'embodied' and 'disembodied' worlds. The dream sequence ends with a brief shot of the twinkling star

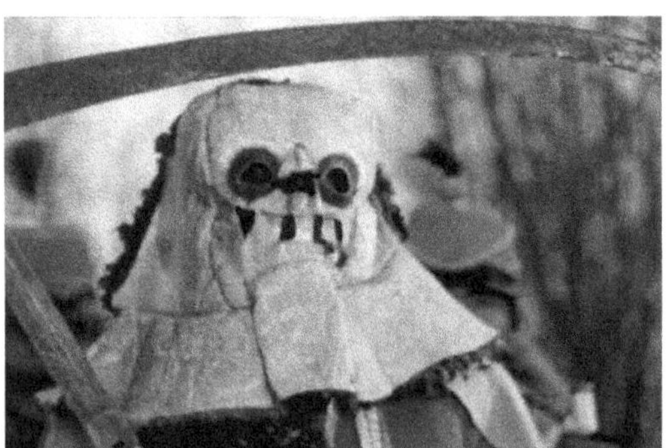

Figure 17: Ivanko as the Grim Reaper. Still from the film.

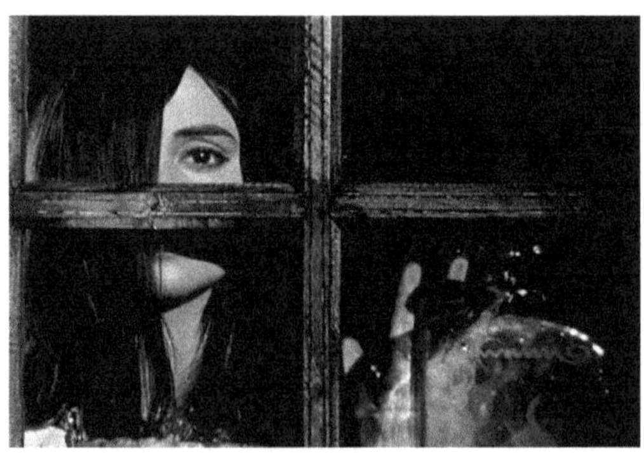

Figure 18: Marichka's apparition in the window. Still from the film.

that warned Ivanko of Marichka's danger, suggesting the return of the apparition that led Marichka to her death. The film cuts back to the vodka and *blinchiki* on the window, and then to Ivanko, who wakes with a start and mutters that 'she's come'. Palahna, still on the bench, turns her head to look out the window, but shrugs and says: 'There's no one there' in her now deep and masculine voice. She tells him to go back to sleep as she removes her apron and covers the window with it. An intertitle tells us: 'Such was life… regular days for work, and holidays for magic…'

Paradjanov does not present Ivanko's new-found superstition and appeal to magic as a normal part of Hutsul everyday life; instead, his dream about Marichka suggests that magic is merely a means to bring the dead back to life. The *blinchiki* and vodka on the window sill are offerings to the spirit world, not merely to protect their sheep but, more importantly, to bring Marichka to him.

'EVE OF SPRING'

Another intertitle tells us that Palahna attempted an offering to Saint Iurii (St. George in English) so he might give her a child. The chapter opens with two close-ups: the first as Ivanko takes his wife's apron away from the window, demonstrating that he has been waiting for a resurrected Marichka to arrive for months; and then to Palahna opening the chest from the wedding scene. She takes a handful of beads out of the chest and looks to her right to make sure Ivanko does not see her. A cut follows to a medium shot of the door as she leaves the house, stripping out of her nightgown into the nude. She turns to the camera and closes the door before the film cuts to a low angle blue-tinted shot of a fence and the sky at dawn. Palahna enters the frame from the right, her naked body partially obscured behind the fence, as smoke rises from below. The camera follows her to the left as she walks along the back side of the crude fence. The low-angle shot is canted as the camera stops and Palahna walks away from it. As her head disappears behind a hill, we notice more smoke rising from the distance. The naked Palahna enters a canvas of hills and ash tree stumps arranged in a circle with three fire pits in the centre, forming a kind of natural temple. She walks to one of the trees in the distance, stopping to prepare her magic, incanting Saint Iurii to bring her a child. The film cuts to Ivanko from above as he washes a horse in a shallow spot on the Cheremosh, and then back to Palahna, this time at eye level. Seemingly as a POV shot, the camera moves up to one of the trees and we see her standing in the distance. Then a hand enters the frame, touching the tree before moving on to the next tree until the same thing happens there. The camera follows this unidentified man, whom we assume to be Ivanko given that the camera's fluid shift between objective and subjective perspective is usually associated with the protagonist. As she prays to Iurii to make Ivanko love her and to grant her 'healthy babies', the camera stops in close-up on her head and shoulders, her face still obscured. Moving slightly around to her profile and pausing at a higher angle, the camera makes her aware of the man. She looks around, just to the left of the camera, and then covers herself with her hands, surprised by his presence, although slightly inviting in her question, 'Haven't you seen a woman before?' The camera arcs down to the ground and then up to reveal the man as the stranger who raped Palahna at Christmas, whose name also happens to be Iurii (usually referred to as 'Iura' in the film), revealing Paradjanov's acute sense of irony. Seen from an extreme low angle, the man grabs her, but she struggles and runs away. The film cuts back to the shot of the fence as she runs the other way, presumably back home. Here again, we should point out the novelty of nudity in Soviet cinema, but also that Tarkovsky used it for a similar purpose two years later in the 'Holiday' chapter of *Andrei Rublev*.

We return to the familiar high-angle long shot from the roof of Ivanko and Palahna's courtyard. Ivanko enters carrying a limp lamb around his neck as Palahna sneaks back inside behind him. As her husband inspects the animal on the ground, she comes out again in a nightgown and they discover that the lamb is ill. This possibly suggests the continued influence of demonic energy on their lives and perhaps proof that Palahna's prayers will not be answered. The sick lamb is also a literal reminder of the fragility of their financial stability and how its loss might impoverish them.[19] Suddenly, the film cuts to the old witch who wailed about her missing children earlier, who now stares directly into the camera as she greets them/us with the traditional 'Praise Jesus', but then cackles hysterically as the film fades

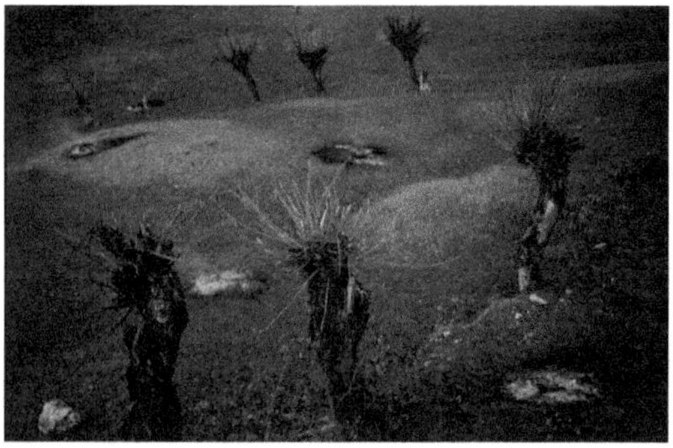

Figure 19: Palahna begins her incantation. Still from the film.

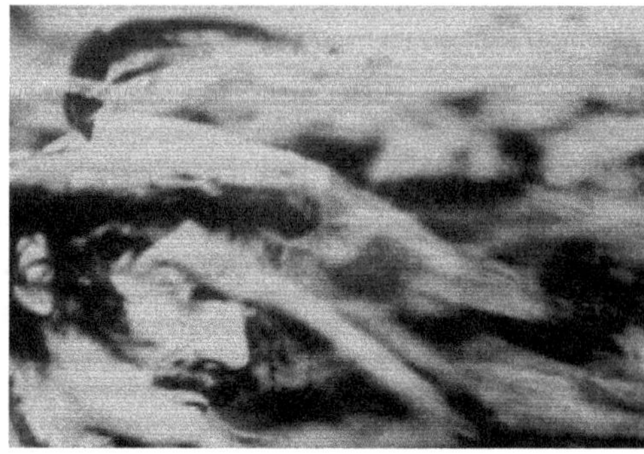

Figure 20: Illienko's trick photography: Iura the sorcerer performing magic. Still from the film.

to red. Grigorian (2011: 97) writes that the presence of the 'old woman seer' foreshadows another movement of a 'dramatic inevitability' in the plot; in this case, the consummation of the illicit relationship between Iura the sorcerer and Palahna, which eventually leads to Ivanko's murder.

'THE SORCERER'

The woman's laughter subsides and we hear the familiar sound of the *drymba*. The intertitle tells us that 'People said that he was like a god. They feared him, but also needed him…'. The film cuts to Palahna, lying on the pasture next to the fence as she plays the instrument, and then away to a close-up of a raven perched on a wooden post. A second close-up shows a wind chime representing a man on horseback, and the third a cow skull. We hear the voice of Palahna's rapist – the sorcerer of the title[20] – uttering an incantation as he picks up the raven, the camera tilting up and then resting on his pockmarked and distorted face. As a storm is brewing, the film returns to Palahna, who gets up from her rest, and then to two horses who attempt to free themselves from their reins and escape for cover. The sorcerer throws rice at the horses as he chants: 'You have no power!' As the sound of lightning strikes, a blurred close-up of the man becomes an infrared freeze-frame that flashes white and orange. Clearly coming from Illienko's bag of tricks, he would also use a tinted infrared and solarisation effect more extensively in his film *Vechir na Ivana Kupala/St. John's Eve* (1968) to delineate a demonic alternate dimension. Here, we find Iura the sorcerer at the intersection of the real and supernatural world. A cut follows to offer a close-up of Palahna as she too tries to dispel the evil forces at work in the storm. Once again, Illienko freezes the frame as it rapidly flashes white and orange several times. The cows scatter with Palahna behind them, and again we see a tinted infrared freeze-frame. Finally, the sorcerer follows on horseback, continuing to ward off evil. The film cuts between Palahna, who herds her cows, and the sorcerer, who rides through the storm uttering his incantation: 'I command you to disappear, to die! I send you there, where no neigh is heard, where a crow cannot fly! Die! Die!' The storm worsens, and the action is barely visible through the windswept dust, leaves and rain. We see a freeze-frame of the horses who flash white and red; the sorcerer then flashes white and orange, as the film continues to cut back and forth between the fleeing horses, the sorcerer, and finally, Palahna's proud face as she utters 'Iurochka'. The affectionate diminutive for the sorcerer contrasts sharply with her abrupt use of 'Ivan' for her husband in the earlier 'Christmas' chapter. A cut introduces another totem of a man on horseback, this one made of bird skulls for the heads of the man and horse. Lightning strikes one of the ravens; we see its fried body falling to the ground before it cuts to Palahna's iconic suggestive look in close-up. Speaking sweetly to him, she turns around to see that he has now fallen onto a bed of large rocks on the ground. He tells her that he has stopped the storm, and sure enough the sound and fury of the wind has died down. A cut follows to her in close-up, now also on the ground, breathing passionately and pulling up her dress, as the camera jerks upward to reveal a lone tree on top of the hill that suddenly bursts into flames. The chapter is a self-contained montage and, with its use of trick photography, asks the audience to accept the sorcerer's magical powers. Whereas Ivanko's and Palahna's incantations are powerless, and nature tends to have an overpowering effect over Hutsuls more generally in the film, Iura successfully commands the storm to stop, and thus represents Palahna's saviour from nature's cruelty in denying her a child.

'THE TAVERN'

As the penultimate chapter title appears on-screen, we hear the *volynky* once again, and then see a crude portrait of the Austrian Emperor Franz Joseph (1830–1916) as an old man surrounded by dried-out corn and homemade totems of men on horseback protecting the monarch from evil spirits. This chapter not only returns us to the conventional narrative of a love triangle, but also historically locates the film in a wider geopolitical and historical space for the first time. The film cuts to a wider shot of the shrine to reveal a flowered wreath around the portrait, and then a medium shot of a Jewish tavern keeper who exchanges traditional greetings with a man off-screen. After the other man – revealed as the *vatah* – throws an animal skin at the Jew, he runs through a door in the rear wall and out come two identical-looking Hasidic boys with two bottles of vodka, dangling pickled herring in front of the camera. The film cuts to a two-shot of identical men at a table, with vodka and appetizers between them. The wall in front of them is a tableau, blank except for an axe stuck to one of the beams, a box full of straw and two hats. The *vatah* enters the frame and sits between the two, facing the camera. At another table, this one with sixteen carousing Hutsuls, both men and women celebrate with two large jugs of wine. The shot resembles Pieter Bruegel's painting 'The Peasant Wedding' (1566–69), which Paradjanov identified in 'Eternal Motion' as one of his influences (Paradzhanov 1966).[21] We hear an off-camera chorus that involves a male/female call and response that continues until the end of the scene. Many of the lines are repeated from the song in the forest, suggesting that we are inside of Ivanko's memory:

> On the other side of the stream
> Straw was burning.
> Come, come to me, young fellow,
> I ache without you.
>
> What kind of ache do you feel,
> Maybe, this is a headache?
> Come, come to me, young fellow,
> At least for an hour.
> And I'll go to the highland pasture
> To that old stable,
> And how will I spend the summer,
> I wonder, I wonder.
> I wonder how to spend the summer,
> How will I pasture my sheep?
> Oh, I'm surely lost...
> ...Without you, my Marichka.
> If you are merciful,
> Forgive my soul.

I shall not grieve,
That I have to sing.
I was in the highland pasture
Got to the river,
Oh, I had it for you, poor little one,
Got frozen as one.
My poor head
Does not want to love.
I will have to go to women
Until I go grey.
Turesh, Turesh,
Oh, my brother, my friend,
I beg you not to betray me,
My dear friend.

Oh, they harassed a woman,
I'm longing for him…
Sweet poor thing,
Many-coloured flower,
If only we fall in love
At least for this summer.
A black mountain, a fine mountain,
One should not to plough it.
We lads easily… [song cuts out as Iura knocks Ivanko unconscious]

The film cuts to an extreme wide-angle shot of a third table, this one with the sorcerer at the far end and the *volynky* player sitting on the right bench. The white walls are bare except for another axe and three hats, making the shot perfectly symmetrical. The sorcerer pours a glass of vodka as the other man plays his *volynky* in exchange for a drink and then leaves the table. A fiddle player enters the frame next with the intention of getting a glass from the wealthy sorcerer, but also leaves after he hands her one. Finally, he stands up and offers a traditional greeting, before the film cuts first to the two Jewish boys sitting on a ladder leading to the top of an absurdly large barrel, and then to Palahna

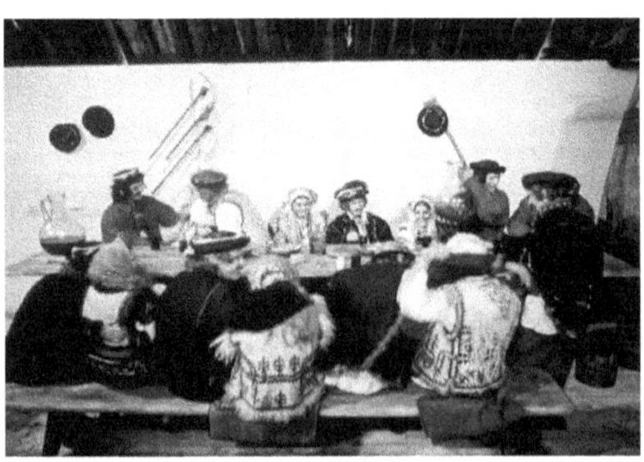

Figure 21: A Hutsul party. Still from the film.

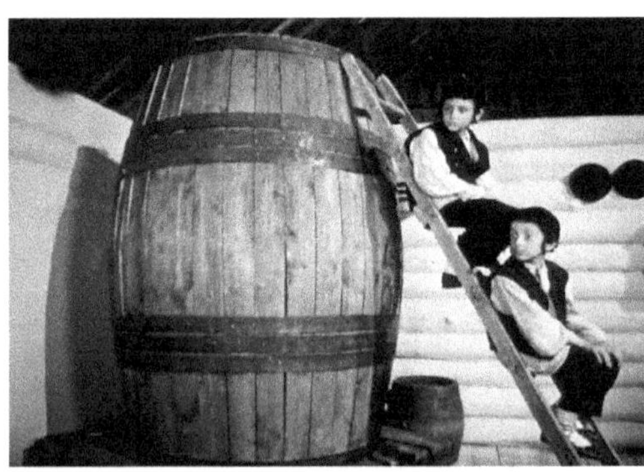

Figure 22: Curious Jewish children in the tavern. Still from the film.

and Ivanko entering the tavern. The former bows to him, but Ivanko merely looks at his wife's rapist and now lover with suspicion. The camera cuts away again to the Jewish boys, who follow the action with synchronized turns of their heads, before returning to the wide shot of the sorcerer, similar to the cutaway to the twin churchmen at the beginning of the film. Ivanko and Palahna sit opposite each other on the close side of the table, as he pours vodka for the two of them. Palahna immediately scoots down to flirt with Iura while two other Hutsuls enter the frame to invite Ivanko to the party at the other table. The camera hovers for a moment on Palahna and Iura embracing each other.

A cut follows to the group where an older Hutsul now assumes the voice of the song playing throughout the scene. In the middle of his chant, Myko rises from the table, noticing something behind him. Another cut takes us to an awkward close-up of the illicit couple; Palahna is now smoking Iura's pipe as they sway back and forth in each other's arms. Myko enters the frame and tries to pry them apart, eventually spitting in the sorcerer's face, and motions Palahna toward her husband. Iura stands with his back to the camera and then punches Myko to the ground, while Palahna calls to Ivanko to intervene. The film cuts back to Ivanko's table as he gets up, and the camera follows him around the tavern, revealing the spatial connection between the various tables for the first time. Ivanko passes the table with the *vatah*, who stands in fearful anticipation of the upcoming fight. As he continues around the tavern, he tries to take another man's axe but, failing that, moves more quickly toward his own, which he has stuck to the other side of Iura's table. As the camera rests on the sorcerer in Ivanko's point of view, with Myko still reeling in pain and Palahna crying next to him, he gets up to grab his axe. Banging the butt against the table threateningly, he lunges toward the camera in an identical move to Hutentiuk's lunge against Paliichuk at the beginning of the film. A close-up follows of Iura's psychotic eyes and distorted face as he swings his axe, connecting to Ivanko's head with the sound of a thump not unlike the film's persistent knock of chopping wood (present before Oleksa's death and in the subsequent scene). The film cuts to an infrared image of Ivanko as he holds his head, the camera slowly spinning around the room with him. The shot moves in slow motion even as the diegetic sound in the scene continues in real time. The camera follows Ivanko back to the entrance; then Ivanko lunges at the camera, the film superimposing multiple stills of him as he gets closer, giving the effect of *palinopsia*.

'IVAN'S DEATH'

The final chapter begins with a medium shot of Ivanko, seen only through slits of light against wooden exterior walls as he stumbles outside of his own yard. We hear an off-camera Iura tell Palahna about the effects of different blows to the human body from an axe. As the camera follows Ivanko, we see the illicit couple inside his and Palahna's courtyard through slits in the fence. From Ivanko's point of view, we see Palahna smoking, laughing with Iura; they chase each other playfully and meet in an embrace, while the camera moves down to reveal Ivanko with his back to the scene.

The film cuts to a high-angle shot as Ivanko stumbles through a burned and cut ash forest, the camera following him from above as he holds his head in pain. Black gradually becomes the dominant colour of the shot, reflecting Ivanko's own decline. We hear a man chanting about giants who once inhabited the earth as a low buzz continues from the end of the previous chapter.

After a cut, there follows an underwater shot, similar to the shot at the end of the 'Routine' chapter. A piece of driftwood splits the frame in two as Ivanko appears on the right side, rinsing his blood-soaked hands. A vision of Marichka (seen as a nymph in Kotsiubyns'kyi's novella) suddenly appears on the other side of the frame, and we hear her song. Both of them move their hands across the top of the water, but then she leaves as Ivanko's song responds to her. A handheld camera moves through the dense forest as Ivanko appears at a clearing in front of a distant rock face. The camera jumps around, cutting at random intervals, and eventually finds both Ivanko and Marichka in close-up. The call and response chant between extra-diegetic male and female voices sing of Marichka's and Ivanko's love cut short:

> Oh, sing, Ivanko,
> Whatever song you know.
> And I will sing for you
> That you won't understand.
>
> Oh, tell me, little girl,
> Where did you take my mind?
> Did you hide in a birch, or in a poplar?
>
> Oh, when we fell in love,
> Withered oaks began to bloom.
> And when we fell apart,
> The grey ones withered,
>
> Oh, sweet Marichka,
> Many-coloured flower,
> If only we could fall in love
> At least for this summer.
>
> Think about me, Ivanko,
> Two times during a day,
> And I will think about you
> Seven times an hour.
> She, sweet, lost her flower,
> As if one fallen from a wreath.
> Both of us fell in love,
> When we were little children,
>
> Oh, I came to the highland pasture,
> And found there a flower.
> What are you up to,
> Dark-haired Marichka?
> Oh my dear Marichka,
> Oh my dear Marichka,
> I cannot forget you…

The film cuts to Ivanko again, who is slowly losing consciousness, and then back to a windswept close-up of Marichka staring into the heavens, as she was when she fell to her death. Marichka looks at the camera as it spins around her, and then back to Ivanko, who asks, as their song ends, 'When shall we be together?' A cut goes back to Marichka, and the camera follows her hands to the left as they grow older and sicklier. At the moment Ivanko's own hand grasps hers, he shouts in pain and the film cuts away to the deer. A montage of strange red and spindly branches appears for several seconds, first spinning and then static, before the chapter ends.

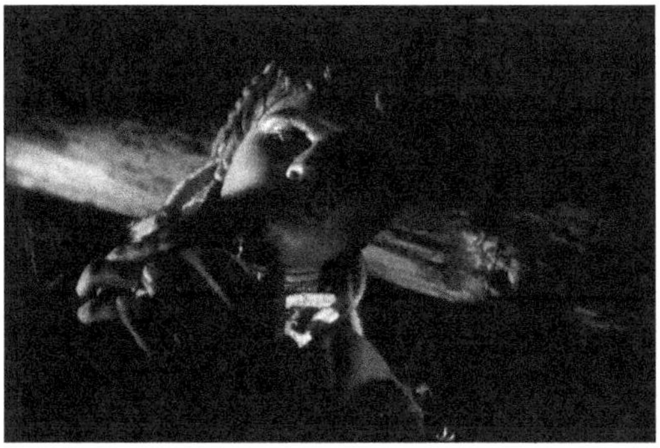

Figure 23: A woman catches an apple at Ivanko's funeral. Still from the film.

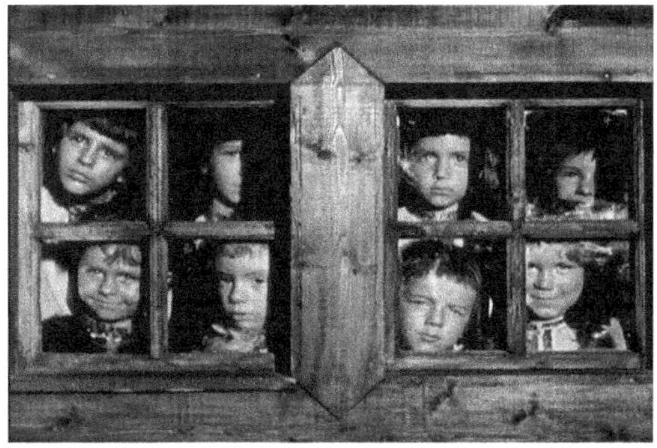

Figure 24: Children's faces in the window panes. Still from the film.

An epilogue is introduced with white letters spelling out 'Pietà' in Latin script against a black screen. A man's cough overlays the cut to a close-up of hands holding a Bible horizontally, open for us to see in a manner that will recall Paradjanov's next film, *The Colour of Pomegranates*. Another hand on the left side of the frame turns the pages to the correct passage as a priest recites funereal prayers. A cut takes us to the location of Ivanko's earlier pre-wedding bath, his body now laid out on a willow board as the same women wash him. A priest recites a benediction as they do so, but the off-camera women (evoking 'Loneliness') complain of the priest's hoarse voice and demand that he drink some vodka to cure it. The film cuts back to the Bible, and then to Palahna, who attaches a silver and pearl necklace around herself, and begins to recite her rehearsed lamentations while swaying disinterestedly. We see a close-up of Ivanko's face surrounded by candles as a *trembita* blares, and then to a medium shot with Myko and two others, who pay their respects by laying an axe on him and dropping coins on his body. The film cuts to a long shot of the room with Ivanko's body and many more Hutsuls sitting, mourning, chanting and observing the body. A low-angle shot follows Palahna around the room as she continues her rehearsed lamentations. Coins continue falling on Ivanko's chest. The tone changes as the *trembita* blares again, and a cut takes us back to a young woman dancing in revelry. The *volynky* player prepares his pipes, old women laugh and dance, Ivanko's body shakes with the commotion as a single woman watches over it with her *floiar*. The *vatah* smokes his pipe in close-up. A low-angle shot spins around the room, surveying the dancing, songs and games, which become increasingly faster and more frantic, the camera eventually revealing a blur of dark colours. This final scene brings together the two essential ethnographic elements of Paradjanov's film – funeral rites and holiday revelry – revealing their profound interconnections, as well as the return of a cyclical narrative mode whereby the dance symbolically serves to 'raise the dead' (Briukhovets'ka 2002: 30; Gazda 1966: 32). An off-camera voice tells us: 'I've just remembered something. Once, while we grazed the sheep, Ivan said to me: "When I die, bury me in the white clothes I wore in my youth". I was surprised when he said that'. The meaning of this short monologue clearly points toward the childhood innocence of his relationship with Marichka.

The film cuts to Ivanko's window frame, this time with a child's face in each pane, and then to a wider shot of the same; there follows a fade to red for the last time to the sound of hammering and conventional symphonic music as credits roll. The final image of *Shadows* is a fitting end as it recalls for us Ivanko's dream on Christmas night, when Marichka's static apparition appears in the window pane. It reiterates the theme of transcendent love associated with childhood, a state that is nonetheless beyond our reach and conflated with lost dreams. Unlike Marichka, however, the children look at us, the viewer, in a final moment of cinematic self-consciousness, wherein the window serves as a metaphor for a screen, offering commentary on the exotic spectacle of 'forgotten ancestors' on display in Paradjanov's film.

Chapter 4
Reception

Very few films have had such a long and involved life as *Shadows of Forgotten Ancestors*, perhaps only comparable to Andrei Tarkovsky's *Andrei Rublev*. In Ukraine, Paradjanov's film became part of a Ukrainian cultural revival, the end of which coincided with his arrest and imprisonment for reasons related both to his open homosexuality and his supposed theft of icons from Hutsul churches during the filming of *Shadows*. Among the film community in Moscow, *Shadows* was understood as the beginning of 'poetic cinema', a movement invented in large part by that very same community, which dominated the critical discourse of the late 1960s and early 1970s. Even though the conversation about 'poetic cinema' in the centre had more to do with aesthetics than nationality, the stakes in this debate too were high, with frequent allusions to the great conflict between formalism and socialist realism during the early 1930s. Paradjanov's film remained at the centre of these debates until the industry and the Communist Party stopped them in the mid-1970s. From the moment the film was released until its erasure from history in 1974, its Soviet reception frequently had a polarizing effect. Internationally, however, the film and its director garnered a small but dedicated following, acquiring the status of a 'cult film' in many ways. Yet its position in the consciousness of the western film community was far overshadowed by the work and personality of Paradjanov's colleague and friend Tarkovsky. Today, *Shadows* remains a fixture in Ukraine, most prominently with a gala to commemorate the 50th anniversary of the September 1965 premiere, which received extensive coverage on the national news, as well as the release in 2013 of a Paradjanov biopic that focuses on his career in the Republic.

BEFORE THE PREMIERE

When *Shadows of Forgotten Ancestors* was released to the general public on 4 September 1965, many people had already seen the film, reviewed it in several newspapers and magazines, and helped maintain interest in it. A day before the Kiev premiere, Goskino issued a warning to its Ukrainian counterpart Derzhkino about free screenings of the film at the October Cultural Centre (Dom kul'tury Oktiabr') (TsDAMLMU 670/1/1852: 178–79). While industry authorities were doubtless concerned about lost revenue, such complaints also pointed to different problems to come with the film's reception. The audience at the October were assuredly members of the Kiev intelligentsia, and individuals who might see in the film as evidence of an emerging Ukrainian cultural renaissance. As such, its value might be transformed into a nationalist rallying point.

Derzhkino passed the completed *Shadows* onto Goskino in Moscow during the autumn of 1964, in the midst of the Kotsiubyns'kyi centenary and a number of retrospectives of earlier film adaptations of the writer's work. The press was proceeding cautiously with Paradjanov's film because it seemed to be caught in bureaucratic limbo for the moment. The Ukrainian Film-makers' Union, however, clearly saw *Shadows of Forgotten Ancestors* as a prestige product that spoke well of the development of Ukrainian culture in recent years. Moreover, Paradjanov's identity as a Tbilisi-born Armenian, educated in Moscow and making Ukrainian cinema affirmed that the 'Friendship of the Peoples'[22] was alive and well in the Sixties' USSR. After taking the film to Tbilisi for the 'Week of Ukrainian Cinema' event, Tymofii Levchuk, the chairman of the Ukrainian Union, reported to his colleagues that *Shadows* had showed the Georgians what national cinema meant (TsDAMLMU 670/1/1750: 147). Georgian film-maker Siko Dolidze (1964: 4) affirmed in the newspaper of the Ukrainian Writers' Union, *Radians'ka kul'tura/Soviet Culture*, that *Shadows* revealed 'an originality of style in Ukrainian cinema'.

In early October 1964, two top Soviet film critics, Inna Solov'eva and Vera Shitova, submitted a glowing review to the main Soviet film journal *Iskusstvo kino*, but it was rejected by the conservative editorial staff and only saw print in 1989. Most likely, the new senior editor of the journal, Evgenii Surkov, feared that Goskino would shelve the film indefinitely, and thus embarrass the magazine in the midst of an increasingly tense relationship between the Soviet intelligentsia and the Communist Party. The specific content of Solov'eva and Shitova's review was unorthodox, but hardly atypical for such Thaw-era critics with an interest in the conflict between entrenched social norms and the figure of the remarkable individual. Yet their analysis of the film ultimately became a vehicle for the authors to promote and critique a new vision of film-making, which they saw on display in *Shadows*. This was a vision that, first of all, questioned the principle of literary verisimilitude in favour of open cinematic interpretation of literature. They wrote that, instead of Kotsiubyns'kyi's 'even tone, [...] the structure of Paradjanov's *Shadows of Forgotten Ancestors* is possessed by a completely alien source of lyrical frenzy, a volatile, ecstatic charge, but which is also strangely fascinating' (Solov'eva and Shitova 1989: 85). Furthermore, Solov'eva and Shitova (1989: 87) claimed that the film provided the tools for 'the theoretical analysis of colour in the cinema, the interrelationship between montage and painting', and several other formal questions pertinent to post-war cinema. In essence, the film was not about a 'reconstruction of the past' or a celebration of the 'shadows of forgotten ancestors', but a message for the contemporary world about the future possibilities of cinema.

At this point, however, the article takes an abrupt turn to sharply criticize Paradjanov's 'souvenir' aesthetic at work in the film, encapsulated not only by his focus on objects and faces (which the viewer can take with them in their memories like a superficial snapshot), but also by the very real objects with which he left Hutsulshchyna, some would say illegally. Solov'eva and Shitova associated this aesthetic with a post-war consumerist mindset, wherein the possession or consumption of foreign cultures stands in for understanding and contextualization. In the end, while artistically groundbreaking, they found *Shadows* to be a 'motionless', 'static' experience (Solov'eva and Shitova 1989: 91).

During late 1964 and early 1965, however, a different problem was developing that kept the film from wider distribution: how to present the film's Carpathian-inflected Ukrainian language on-screen. Standard practice in the Soviet film industry required a dubbed Russian version for all-Union and international release, even though studios in the Republic were also encouraged to make their films in the vernacular. Paradjanov believed translation was impossible in light of the aural texture of the film, which included numerous local folk songs and a heavy use of the Carpathian dialect of Ukrainian. According to Paradjanov and many of his supporters at the studio, dubbing it into literary Russian would have eroded its all-important authenticity. Sviatoslav Ivanov agreed to a compromise, writing to Goskino that the 'rich folkloric material [...] cannot yield a translation into Russian', and asked them to accept a Russian-subtitled version instead (RGALI 2944/4/280: 26). Such a request was indeed unprecedented in the Soviet Union, and was clearly influenced by emerging practices in some West European countries, such as France, Sweden and the United Kingdom, in addition to the United States. Italy, West Germany and others continued to dub each voice separately in foreign-language films, but the Soviet Union and its satellites used the unique and indeed primitive practice of single-voice dubbing. Essentially, the studio would reduce the volume of the original dialogue so that it remains barely audible and then overdub a single voice in the new language for the entire dialogue. While audiences unaccustomed to such a practice find it frustrating and awkward to watch Russian-dubbed films, Soviet spectators flocked to foreign movies without any concern that it would detract from their experience.

Moreover, the Ukrainian studio invested thousands of roubles every year needlessly dubbing Russian films into Ukrainian based on the principles of Soviet nationalities policy. After all, over 90 per cent of Ukrainians knew at least some Russian by the 1960s. The studio itself continually had problems hiring actors who knew Ukrainian and, closer to the point at issue, the studio had to find someone to overdub one actor's dialogue in *Shadows* who did not know a word of the 'authentic' language of the film (TsDAMLMU 670/1/1750: 205). Apparently, Goskino rejected this unprecedented idea to subtitle the entire film, but agreed to a follow-up suggestion for Russian-language explanatory intertitles while still maintaining the Ukrainian dialogue (RGALI 2944/4/280: 27; TsDAMLMU 670/1/1581: 16, 19).

Nonetheless, the film remained at Goskino in Moscow while the Ukrainian Film-makers' Union continued to screen it for select audiences in Kiev. December saw two more positive reviews appear in the Ukrainian press, one in *Novyny kinoekrana/News from the Screen*, a popular film magazine owned and edited by the Union, and a second in *Radians'ka kul'tura* featuring Ivan Mykolaichuk. The latter article established Mykolaichuk as a genuine object of the Carpathian exotic. The author wrote: 'The actor found himself in the fairy-tale Carpathian land – dear to his soul – both legs standing on Hutsul land with the cries of the shepherds, sounds of the *trembita* and little girls singing' (Korobchak 1964: 4; Musiienko 1964: 4–5). At this point, Goskino summoned Paradjanov to Moscow to discuss the film during a special meeting of the Soviet Film-makers' Union. The director found himself in front of a rapt audience, showered with praise from both the older generation of Soviet film-makers and young upstarts (RGALI 2936/1/528).

This overwhelming support for Paradjanov's film and for the director's refusal to make a Russian dub must have had an effect on Goskino, as Oleksandr Syzonenko wrote a Russian press release for the film at the end of the year emphasizing both the positive ethnographic texture of the film and the authenticity of Mykolaichuk's portrayal of Ivanko: 'He does not perform, but lives in this image' (TsDAMLMU 670/1/1581: 21). During the following week, two positive reviews were featured in the high-circulation central newspapers *Komsomol'skaia Pravda/Komsomol's Pravda* (Turbin 1964: 4) and *Uchitel'skaia gazeta/Teachers' Gazette* (Petrovskii 1964: 4). On 8 January, Derzhkino seemed to have ended the dubbing controversy by asking Paradjanov to supervise the Russian version (TsDAMLMU 670/1/1856: 8). The following month, Vladimir Turbin (1965: 280), the critic who wrote the first review in *Komsomol'skaia Pravda*, expanded upon the film in *Molodaia gvardiia/The Young Guard*, a 'thick journal' for young people, where he claimed that 'geniuses' had made *Shadows*. Later in the month, poet and Paradjanov collaborator Ivan Drach (1965: 17) wrote a review in *Literaturnaia Rossiia/Literary Russia* with the explicit title: 'Thank You!' And during a Ukrainian Film-makers' Union Plenum in March, First Secretary Levchuk reiterated his praise for the film, saying that it represented a 'creative victory' for Dovzhenko Studios and a 'turning point' in Ukrainian cinema (TsDAMLMU 655/1/310: 13). The Ukrainian film community had reached a consensus that *Shadows of Forgotten Ancestors* had fulfilled its promise to resurrect Ukraine's negative reputation. It had reversed decades of negative press about the Kiev Studio, vindicated Ivanov and Tsvirkunov, and affirmed Shelest's role as a supporter of native-language Ukrainian culture.

Nonetheless, the dubbing controversy refused to fade away, in part because Paradjanov refused to fulfil his end of the bargain in the production of the Russian version. Romanov's deputy at Goskino, Vladimir Baskakov, wrote to the Ukrainian leadership that he expected a Russian voice-over commentary in between the various sections of the film, whereas Paradjanov only offered a series of intertitles (TsDAMLMU 670/1/1829: 44). Ironically, *Kul'tura i zhyttia/Culture and Life* (the new title of *Radians'ka kul'tura*) published an article praising Goskino for accepting Paradjanov's Russian version at the very moment that the issue had flared up again between the Ukrainians and Moscow authorities (Adrianova 1965: 4).

As the film was still on hold for domestic distribution, *Shadows* had been accepted for the Mar del Plata International Film Festival in Argentina. While authorities forbade Paradjanov from attending, Ivanov took Mykolaichuk and Kadochnikova to the festival, where they presented the film and accepted the Southern Cross Award for it. Mykolaichuk would relate his experiences in Mar del Plata in April, writing that the audience was filled with Ukrainian émigrés who flocked to *Shadows* to get a glimpse of their 'native land'. Thus, the film also served a very specific propagandistic function: to sell Soviet Ukraine to the largely anti-Soviet diaspora (Anon 1965: 4; Mykolaichuk 1991). Nonetheless, the accolades in Argentina were a double-edged sword. While festival participation allowed the film-makers to use the event to pressurize the authorities to release the film on the big screen, detractors saw Mar del Plata as evidence that the film was more for the West than for Soviet spectators.

After several major reviews in the central press and other Union-sponsored screenings, including one in the Kazakh capital of Alma-Ata in June and another in East Berlin in August, Goskino finally accepted the Russian version with some unobtrusive voice-over (later excised for international release), but largely done according to Paradjanov's own specifications. The premiere was scheduled for 4 September, during the annual Cinema Days festival in Kiev, organized by the Ukrainian Film-makers' Union.

THE PREMIERE AND INITIAL THEATRICAL RUN OF *SHADOWS OF FORGOTTEN ANCESTORS*

Despite the seemingly unanimously positive response from critics and Paradjanov's colleagues, several earlier events suggested that the authorities needed to be vigilant for problems with the film's reception. Throughout the early 1960s, students at Kiev State University spoke about the condition of Ukraine as a 'colonized' nation, and in 1962, a literature professor gave voice to such concerns with a public lecture on the poor state of the Ukrainian language in higher education (Lewytzkyj 1984: 67). Moreover, the Taras Shevchenko statue in the park adjacent to the university served as a rallying spot for students, artists and intellectuals concerned about these issues (TsDAHOU 1/24/6160: 104). In effect, the figure of the nineteenth-century Ukrainian national poet was being reappropriated by non-conformists and dissidents in the same way as the statue of Pushkin was in Moscow around this time. At the end of August 1965, the Ukrainian branch of the KGB arrested about a dozen West Ukrainian activists on charges of 'bourgeois nationalism', sending tremors throughout the Kiev intelligentsia. Much of this activism and criticism of the authorities in Ukraine had to do with language. The delay in the release of *Shadows* also concerned language, although Paradjanov's conflict with Goskino was admittedly for different reasons. Thus, local and industry authorities were concerned that the film could serve as another rallying point for the nationalist elements of the Ukrainian intelligentsia. The concern was all the more ominous to ideological watchdogs in the Communist Party of Ukraine like Andrii Skaba, because his immediate superior, First Secretary Shelest, seemed to give voice to the same concerns driving a nascent movement toward Ukrainianization in the Republic.

Nonetheless, the decision to premiere *Shadows* as part of the 6th Annual Cinema Days meant that the Film-makers' Union was in charge of the event. That year, the Union planned a number of premieres, receptions with actors and directors open to the general public, and other events that they expected would attract hundreds of thousands of visitors over the weekend of 4–6 September. Although the Cinema Days featured films from around the Soviet Union, the Film-makers' Union brought to the event their own agenda to promote Ukrainian cinema in particular. Consequently, the promotional materials and press releases all featured the Dovzhenko Studios' productions more prominently than even the most well-known of the central productions. The weekly newspaper *Na ekranakh Kyieva/On Kiev's Screens* made no mention of anything but Ukrainian films in its Cinema Days feature on 28 August. Moreover, the front page featured photographs of Paradjanov and Mykolaichuk along with a still from *Shadows*. Clearly, Union planners intended the film's premiere on Saturday night to be the main attraction of the entire weekend, regardless of what audiences might have thought of such a strange film, or of the fears that Party authorities might have had. In the end, the Cinema Days festival was a huge box-office success, with 340,000 people seeing films over the course of the weekend. The *Shadows* premiere, however, was a political disaster with far-reaching consequences.

It was a natural decision to allow the director to introduce the film at the modern and centrally located Ukraina cinema, even though Goskino forbade him to accompany the film to Argentina in the spring. They were also apprehensive about letting the difficult director participate in a Kiev television broadcast the night before the premiere that featured Levchuk, Tsvirkunov, and a number of other prominent Ukrainian directors and actors. Even before the premiere started, problems emerged because tickets had sold out long before 4 September. As one attendee later recounted, the Union had distributed complimentary tickets to the many members of the Kiev intelligentsia who were friends with the cast and crew, perhaps to assuage fears that *Shadows* would not bring viewers into the cinema and thus embarrass the Union (personal communication with Svetlana Petrovskaia, June 2006). Yet with the massive promotion of the film, not only for Cinema Days, but also with the extensive coverage and reviews in the Ukrainian press during the previous year, viewers were understandably curious about it. When the box office turned them down, several members of the public forced their way in to the cinema, either through the lobby entrance or even through windows (TsDAMLMU 655/1/309: 243–47). Later, Ivanov would try to deflect blame for this to the Kiev Municipal Administration for Cultural Affairs for poor organization, but the Union ultimately had to accept responsibility and later took a smaller role in Cinema Days. The larger problem emerged when Paradjanov took the stage at 8 p.m. to introduce his film alongside the film's costume designer, Lidiia Baikova. The manager of the Ukraina cinema later reported to Ivanov that Paradjanov used this opportunity to air his grievances about the film's delayed release, and said that 'blacks, the French and the Argentines understand the film, but the organs [of distribution] won't allow the film to be released [here], on the grounds that our people won't understand it'. Paradjanov also spoke about the now-settled dubbing controversy, bragging that he stood his ground so that the film would not 'lose it national colour' (Brainchenko 2001: 268).

Such 'demagoguery', as the cinema manager Fedir Brainchenko put it, provided the ideological justification for the 'anti-Soviet' action that followed. After finishing his speech, literary critic and niece of Kotsiubyns'kyi, Mykhailyna Kotsiubyns'ka, presented flowers to Paradjanov while Ivan Dziuba, an editor of the newspaper *Literaturna Ukraina/Literary Ukraine*, presented flowers to Baikova. Dziuba grabbed the microphone from the director and shouted to the audience: 'The reaction of 1937 [the Stalinist Terror] has returned to Ukraine. The best of the Ukrainian intelligentsia in Kiev and L'vov are being arrested. Shame on those in power. Whoever wants to protest against the terror – stand up!' According to an eyewitness, only a few members of the audience stood up. In his report to the Ukrainian Council of Ministers, Ivanov referred to them as 'rough-necks' (TsDAVOU 4754/1/50: 65–66). Brainchenko reported that most members of the audience instead shouted at Dziuba to get off the stage, but Svetlana Petrovskaia, who attended the screening, did not remember any such reaction to Dziuba's action (personal correspondence June 2006). Brainchenko (2001: 268) then 'tore the microphone from the political hooligan's hand' and two minutes later the screening began (TsDAVOU 4754/1/50: 65). Afterwards, Dziuba, along with the poet Vasyl' Stus and the known dissident Viacheslav Chornovil, tried to rally the viewers once again, but they were still unwilling to participate, largely because of the large police presence now around the Ukraina. While the action stopped short of a mass public disturbance, Mykolaichuk later recalled his shock at the violent treatment of the police toward the few individuals who participated (Hoseiko 2005: 190). Moreover, the event seemed to confirm exactly what Party and industry authorities had feared: that Paradjanov would behave inappropriately and that Ukrainian nationalists would (re)appropriate the text for their own purposes.

The following day, the film was slotted for another screening, but distribution authorities cancelled it (TsDAMLMU 655/1/317: 16). On the following Thursday, the Presidium of the Ukrainian Film-makers' Union summoned Paradjanov to apologize for his speech and to interrogate him about any involvement with the subsequent protest. Instead, the director continued to complain about the Russian dub and the hold-up in distribution. Nonetheless, he made sure to disassociate himself from the protest, and proclaimed: 'I am a Soviet man and do not agree with Dziuba. I am indignant at Dziuba's conduct [...]'. At the same time, he turned his statement around and continued: 'I think that if he really was our enemy, he would not have openly spoken this way'. In essence, while Paradjanov does not claim an affinity with Dziuba's ideas, he nonetheless accepted his right to air them at his premiere. Instead, Paradjanov concerned himself with the true problem at the event, namely the poor organization that allowed unticketed spectators to disrupt a film premiere intended for the intelligentsia. In fact, Paradjanov complained about the lack of intellectuals in the audience and the presence of '50 children' instead (TsDAMLMU 655/1/309: 243–47). The same day, *Kul'tura i zhyttia* reported on Cinema Days with praise for the turnout and the myriad of great films at the event. The author did not so much as mention *Shadows of Forgotten Ancestors* (Zorin 1965: 4). The film sat in limbo, perhaps too dangerous for the authorities to release to the general public for fear of similar situations, or perhaps to punish Paradjanov for his loose lips.

A week later, however, it reappeared in print. Evhen Kyryliuk reviewed the film for *Literaturna Ukraina*, defending it as a definitive work of socialist realism. While admitting the film's complexity, he argued that it functioned within a new conception of socialist realism, one that emerged after the Stalinist 'cult of personality'. He went on to write:

> We had heard the discussion about *Shadows of Forgotten Ancestors* from comrades who were lucky enough to watch it during the previous year. And so I watched the film with some apprehension. With sober consideration, you come to the conclusion that the screenwriters correctly read Kotsiubyns'kyi's story [...]. In my opinion, Sergei Paradjanov's film is a work of Socialist Realism. The essential progressive [plot] lines of M. Kotsiubyns'kyi have been preserved in it: The amazing and beautiful Hutsul nature, the vigorous and powerful human characters.
>
> (Kyryliuk 1965: 3)

The film was not only a work of beauty, but also contained a socially acceptable plot. On Monday 20 October, *Shadows of Forgotten Ancestors* returned to the Ukraina for a one-night test screening. When that went well, they began to hold nightly screenings until 17 October, after which point the film entered broad circulation until the end of the month, before tapering off until the end of the first week of November. At that point, *Shadows* entered the secondary market of factory club screenings until the end of November. While not comparable to the broad circulation of the historical-revolutionary epic *Hadiuka/The Viper* (Ivchenko, 1966), which screened throughout Kiev during the entire summer of 1966, *Shadows* held its own at the cinema for the limited release it had.

Throughout its run during the autumn of 1965, critics and fellow film-makers heaped praise on *Shadows*. Dmytro Shlapak (1965: 1) glowed that spectators will want to see the film a second or third time. Levchuk spoke about the 'revelation of the national originality of culture, everyday life, language, and customs of our people' in the film. Ivanov, however, noted in a Ukrainian Film-makers' Union meeting that spectators judged the film harshly (TsDAMLMU, 655/1/313: 109). And indeed, an oft-referenced letter from one A. Mikhalev from Dnepropetrovsk wrote, 'If you wish to know what happened to me during a screening of *Shadows of Distant* [*dalekikh*, sic] *Ancestors*, take a bowl of good Ukrainian borshch, put a half kilo of honey in it and try to eat it within a half an hour [...]. That will tell you about the condition of my brain during the next day [...]' (TsDAMLMU 670/1/1829: 1). He continued: 'For the first time in my life, I saw spectators, not by themselves, but in rows, who got up and left' (TsDAMLMU 670/1/1829: 3). Typical of its detractors in Ukraine, the film was defined as a failure for its lack of a proper Ukrainian consciousness, rather than for any formal errors.

SHADOWS OF FORGOTTEN ANCESTORS AND THE CULTURE WARS OF THE LATE 1960S AND EARLY 1970S

The second half of the 1960s, both in Ukraine and in the Soviet Union more generally, were marked by a series of culture wars that ultimately ended in a clampdown on dissent following the invasion of Czechoslovakia in August 1968. In October 1964, the Central Committee of the Communist Party ousted Khrushchev for a number of reasons other than his approach to culture or nationality issues. But the clampdown on the Ukrainian intelligentsia in August and September 1965 coincided with the arrest of writers Andrei Siniavskii and Iulii Daniel' for publishing anti-Soviet material abroad. On 5 December, activists in Moscow began their annual Constitution Day protests on Pushkin Square against the government's human rights abuses. At Dovzhenko Studios, Iurii Illienko directed his first film, based on a screenplay by Ivan Drach, called *A Well for the Thirsty*, which was shelved by the end of 1966 for its opaque and potentially subversive symbolism. Party member Drach's political credibility was questioned further when he participated in an April protest in L'vov against the trial of the L'vov Ten – those arrested before the *Shadows* premiere (TsDAHOU 1/24/6160: 11–14, 61, 63, 95, 110). In November, First Secretary Petro Shelest spoke at the 5th Congress of Ukrainian Writers to resounding applause when he demanded more literature in the Ukrainian language and bemoaned the continued Russification of education in the Republic. By the end of the year, Ivan Dziuba would seek foreign publishers for his political tract *Internatsionalizm chy russifikatsiia?/ Internationalism or Russification?*, an excoriation of the incomplete and contradictory implementation of Soviet nationalities policy. Shelest reiterated his points about the use of Ukrainian in literature and education when a group of Canadian communists came to visit Ukraine the following April, just before the Montreal Expo (Krawchenko 1985: 201). In January 1968, the Ukrainian literary journal *Vitchyzna* began publishing the divisive novel *Sobor/The Church* by Ukrainian Writers' Union First Secretary Oles' Honchar, which told a story of a small industrial town whose church symbolizes a lost sense of community. The novel caused an uproar, both in support of its traditionalist message, and against its supposed fetish of backward values and anti-Party message. In a sense, the battle lines had already been drawn around *Shadows* and Honchar's book merely reaffirmed those positions. Eventually, the head of the Dnepropetrovsk Party Committee got the novel banned and the KGB confiscated extant copies of the journal (Koval' 1993). At the same time, 1968 saw the appointment of Fedir Ovcharenko as Ideological Secretary of the Communist Party of Ukraine in place of hardliner Andrii Skaba, a clear sign of a cultural thaw coming from Shelest. Party authorities admitted they were 'overzealous' in their campaign again Honchar, but then called for Dziuba's expulsion from the Writers' Union (with Honchar's support) for publishing abroad. Shelest himself, who agreed with Dziuba's ideas if not his tactics, published a positive assessment of pre-Revolutionary Ukrainian history and culture in 1970, but then commented harshly on writers' and artists' recent critiques of Russification a year later at the 24th Congress of the CPU (Shelest 1970). Clearly, the First Secretary was trying to balance his own principles with the growing movement to clamp down on Ukrainianization, the latter led by CPU secretaries Volodymyr Shcherbyts'kyi and Valentyn Malanchuk. In May 1972, the Central Committee of the CPU ousted Shelest and elected Shcherbyts'kyi as First Secretary. In October, Shelest's supporters were purged from the CPU, and cultural politics in the Republic took a definitive turn away from Ukrainianization, now moving toward acceptance of Russification in the arts and education. Two years later, Shcherbyts'kyi made a direct critique of 'Ukrainian poetic cinema', which shut down any new productions based on pre-Revolutionary Ukrainian historical or folkloric material. By this time, Sergei Paradjanov was serving a seven-year prison sentence, and the comments by the new First Secretary made his name and work unmentionable in Ukraine.

The beginning of 1966 brought both positive and negative assessments for a film that only grew in importance after its run at the cinema ended. The first issue of *Iskusstvo kino* gave us Paradjanov's 'Eternal Motion' (discussed in Chapter 3), which became one of the most widely read articles that year. Apart from an exploration of his aesthetic principles, it also attempted to fit his film into a recent history of Ukrainian cinema and its use of native folkloric traditions. Yet the impression that Paradjanov's detractors took from 'Eternal Motion' was its celebration of an eclectic and cosmopolitan selection of western, eastern and Russian painters that included not only the acceptably realist artists in the tradition of the Wanderers, but also the Dutch Renaissance, the impressionism of the Japanese Rinpa school of the seventeenth and eighteenth centuries, Russian Symbolism, Cubism and Primitivism. Absent from his list of influences was any painter in the socialist-realist tradition, nor did Paradjanov mention any writers from the Soviet canon.

On 5 January, a group of important Communist Party, state and studio representatives met at Dovzhenko Studios to discuss the possibility of nominating *Shadows of Forgotten Ancestors* for the Shevchenko State Prize, the most prestigious award for a work of Ukrainian art and literature. Viktor Ivchenko (director of *The Viper* and dean of the Kiev film school) had initially nominated Paradjanov's film on behalf of the Union, which was generally a cut-and-dry process. However, the influential playwright and apparatchik of the Communist Party of Ukraine, Oleksandr Korniichuk, refused to allow the film to be considered. During the meeting, he closed the door on the film, stating:

> For Argentines who saw *Shadows of Forgotten Ancestors*, it was important how the cinematographer makes the trees spin around so that your head hurts, but we Ukrainians, when we examine such a mutilated face of the Ukrainian people, it's not pleasant for us. There are certain wild tendencies there. It's not the Ukrainian people. This film has nothing in common with Kotsiubyns'kyi.
>
> (Blokhin 2002: 69)

Despite several protests from prominent film-makers, screenwriters and Ivanov himself about the film's contribution to Ukrainian culture, Korniichuk killed the nomination. And when the Ukrainian Film-makers' Union tried to nominate the film again in 1967, Levchuk rejected it on the basis that it could not be nominated twice (TsDAMLMU 655/1/395: 155). After this key January 1966 meeting, we begin to see a shift – subtle at first – against the film's positive reception among Ukraine's opinion-makers.

Nonetheless, film critics were just as celebratory as ever during 1966. Oleh Babyshkin's book *Ukrainian Literature on the Screen* (1966) praised *Shadows*, drawing attention to the story's reinvention and 're-embodiment' through cinema. Dmytro Shlapak (1966: 1) wrote in March that Dovzhenko's influence on Ukrainian cinema is revealed most clearly in Paradjanov's film. These two pieces answered two complaints about *Shadows of Forgotten Ancestors*: first, that the film was not a literary adaptation at all, and instead expressed the very personal aesthetic principles of an eccentric outsider to Ukrainian culture; and second, that the influence of Kiev Studio's namesake was in fact in the realm of socialist realism and not 'poetic cinema'.

The film continued to screen in Kiev, typically for a few weeks in the spring every year until the end of the decade. *Shadows* came to the Druzhba Cinema on Kreshchatik in central Kiev in mid-March for a long weekend, and was then included in competition for the Second All-Union Film Festival in May, which happened to be in Kiev that year. In the midst of the festival, members of the Ukrainian Film-makers' Union complained that *Shadows* was not getting the attention it deserved. Nonetheless, it received distinction for a 'Talented Artistic Search and Innovation', perhaps more of a consolation prize than an acknowledgment of its specific accomplishments (Anon 1966a: 4).

Shadows continued to perform well at international film festivals and at rare screenings abroad. The French magazine *Cinéma* published a review in September 1966 after the film screened as part of a 'Week of Ukrainian Culture in France' (Shnitseri and Zhan 1966: 6). And the famous *New York Times* critic Bosley Crowther (1966: 39) wrote about it briefly when he saw it at the New York International Film Festival in September, calling it an 'unusual Ukrainian film', the whole significance of which lies in its 'brilliant reproduction of ancient customs and traditional sentiment'. The *New York Post* was nicer to the film, and its review appeared translated in *Kul'tura i zhyttia* the following week (Anon 1966b: 3). In 1967, the film screened at the popular USSR Pavilion for 'Ukraine Day' at the Montreal Expo, demonstrating its role of representing the Republic in the politically sensitive space of Canada, with its large and politically active Ukrainian émigré population (TsDAVOU 4754/1/78: 1). Officials within Derzhkino and at Dovzhenko Studios, along with Ukrainian film-makers themselves, drew attention to the film's international success at every moment they could. Levchuk, however, wondered aloud at a January 1967 meeting of the Soviet Film-makers' Union in Moscow why, with the exception of Mar del Plata, such screenings abroad all took place without the participation of members of the cast and crew (RGALI 2936/4/68: 13). The First Secretary of the Ukrainian Union identified a fear that industry authorities had of the crew, perhaps of Paradjanov in particular, who, after the premiere, was considered somewhat of a loose cannon: what would he say to foreign reporters, they wondered?

The same January meeting was dedicated to the 'Problems of National Cinema', and featured a keynote address by the famous Kirghiz novelist and screenwriter Chinghiz Aitmatov. While Aitmatov's talents had been lent to a few recent 'poetic' films made in Soviet Kirghizia, such as Larisa Shepit'ko's *Znoi*/*Heat* (1963) and Andrei Konchalovskii's

Pervyi uchitel'/The First Teacher (1964), and he was himself a fan of an ethnographic style of representation, the writer did not treat *Shadows of Forgotten Ancestors* well. Aitmatov told the Union delegates that the film contains 'no dramaturgy. It's like a verse, it's poetic [...]. But nevertheless, it can't be said that it lies in the mainstream of contemporary national cinema' (RGALI 2936/4/67: 48). He concluded that, with all its beauty, '*Shadows of Forgotten Ancestors* carries a relatively limited message to our day' (RGALI 2936/4/67: 48). Levchuk protested, saying: 'The Ukrainian landscape, songs and customs, the costumes were all subordinated to the most important thing – the revelation in dramatic conflict, I repeat, of genuinely national characters' (RGALI 2936/4/68: 13). This debate between the limited significance of *Shadows* – that it was just about pretty things – and its broader importance for 'national cinema' (or even Soviet cinema) remained essential for the rest of the film's life in the USSR.

After returning home to Kiev, Levchuk tried to spin Aitmatov's critique into a compliment during a meeting of the Ukrainian union, and drew attention once again to the film's positive use of Ukrainian folklore (TsDAMLMU 655/1/400: 10). At the same meeting in March, however, the ideological watchdog within both the Ukrainian Film-makers' and Writers' Unions, Oleksandr Levada, criticized the film for having a 'limited resonance with the spectator', pointing toward a 'peculiar disproportion between the form and content of the film' (TsDAMLMU 655/1/400: 153). Aping Aitmatov, Levada complained of the lack of psychological depth to the protagonists. Finally, in drawing attention to Paradjanov's widely-read article 'Eternal Motion', Levada complained that painting offers a pale comparison to cinematography, and that the director should have emphasized its relation to drama (TsDAMLMU 655/1/400: 153). Levada's statements demonstrated that the points of contention about the film were slowly moving outside the realm of its significance for Ukraine or 'national cinema' by increasingly touching upon questions of film form and audience politics. *Shadows* screened a few times in March and April at the Druzhba Cinema, but two letters published in the June issue of *Novyny kinoekrana* revealed much the same critique as Aitmatov and Levada: the film offers no lessons for the contemporary world, and it is too concerned with beauty to the detriment of drama. Whereas the editors refused to print Mikhalev's letter from the previous year (perhaps because his overt anti-Ukrainian bias was politically incorrect), the self-described Hutsul Bohdan Chufus wrote:

> Dovzhenko Studios gave us *Shadows of Forgotten Ancestors* [...] but this event was in the past! We would like to see contemporary Hutsuls, who approach the glory of communism with their labour. We are waiting, dear film-makers, for films about the contemporary Carpathians from you.
>
> (Chufus 1967: 4)

The next site of contestation about the film was a collection of essays about Ukrainian cinema published in 1968. While the editor of *Fil'm i doba/Film and Our Era*, Ivan Korniienko, wrote positively about *Shadows*, another essay by Mykhailo Solomonov opined that the film was 'aesthetically cold' with its 'motif of solitude'. Moreover, he questioned whether an 'ethnography' should really be exemplary of the 'national form of Ukrainian cinema [...]. In *Shadows*, S. Paradjanov wonderfully and originally combined the most effective means in order to paint a vivid picture of the past. [But] the authors got carried away by this past' (Korniienko 1968: 68; 90). Then, in the March issue of *Mystetstvo/Art*, film critic Poltarats'kyi (1968: 35) wrote that there was 'little of Kotsiubyns'kyi's content' in Paradjanov's film. Granted, by this time, Paradjanov had already left Ukraine for Armenia after Goskino shut down his next film, *Kyiv Frescoes*, and was in the midst of another fight regarding his Armenfil'm production *Saiat-Nova* (which later became *Colour of Pomegranates*), which threatened to transform him into a permanent persona non grata.

Through this process, the director maintained a large group of friends and disciples in Kiev. During a March 1968 meeting of the Dovzhenko Studios' creative staff, for example, Shlapak proclaimed to enthusiastic applause that Ukraine should confer upon Paradjanov the distinction of Honoured Artist (TsDAMLMU 670/1/2159: 46). At a conference celebrating the 50th anniversary of Ukrainian cinema in April 1969, one participant once again identified *Shadows* within a grand tradition of Ukrainian auteurs like Dovzhenko (TsDAMLMU 655/1/501: 8).

Much of this conflict over *Shadows* was a microcosm of the culture wars happening within Ukraine in the late 1960s, but the Prague Spring and the subsequent Warsaw Pact invasion of Czechoslovakia in August 1968 brought these conflicts into the broader framework of the autonomy of national culture on one side, and the implicit cultural and political hierarchy contained in the Brezhnev Doctrine on the other. Paradoxically, it was a combination of Paradjanov's cosmopolitanism, along with his connections to Ukrainian nationalists like Dziuba and others, that led to his arrest in December 1973. But the real debate about *Shadows of Forgotten Ancestors* in Moscow was among film critics whose concerns, both positive and negative, about a visual turn in Soviet cinema added another layer to the charges against the director.

MIKHAIL BLEIMAN'S INTERVENTION AND THE SILENCING OF *SHADOWS*

In July 1970, *Iskusstvo kino* published Mikhail Bleiman's article 'Arkhaisty ili novatory?' /'Archaicists or Innovators?', which opened the final stage of the Soviet debate about *Shadows of Forgotten Ancestors*. Bleiman was a veteran screenwriter and film critic, whose career went back to the 1920s. Since the late 1950s, Goskino had contracted him to write internal reviews of questionable scripts. He had read and critiqued Iurii Illienko's surreal adaptation of Nikolai Gogol's *St. John's Eve* in 1967, and was well-versed on recent trends in both Ukrainian and Georgian cinemas. The Goskino management team – Aleksei Romanov, Vladimir Baskakov and Aleksandr Karaganov – trusted Bleiman's opinions completely, and he consequently had the power to make or break film-makers' careers. He was also highly intelligent, and knowledgeable about the history of cinema, cultural theory, and Thaw-era debates about aesthetics and cultural politics.

'Archaicists or Innovators?' began with a highly positive treatment of *Shadows of Forgotten Ancestors*, calling Paradjanov's film an 'incredibly talented picture' that mixed the tragedy of the 'Romeo and Juliet' plot with the 'bright and life-affirming character' of the Hutsuls (Bleiman 1973: 507–08). The question was not, however, whether *Shadows* accomplished its goals, because Bleiman answered this affirmatively; rather, he questioned whether such aesthetic principles were acceptable in Soviet cinema. In identifying several 'failed' works of poetic cinema as the now-forgotten Ukrainian film *Zaivyi khlib/Left-Over Bread* (Hoviada, 1966), along with the central production *The Arena* (Samsonov, 1967), he slowly conflated them with *Shadows* itself, and cast doubt on the very film that he initially praised. As he argued: 'One important film is not much, with which to define the principles of a new poetics' (Bleiman 1973: 512). Later, when discussing the work of Illienko and another Ukrainian director Leonid Osyka, Bleiman (1973: 515) got to his main point: 'In recalling the principles of S. Paradjanov's poetics, it becomes clear that this is not only an influence, but also a unity of a creative and aesthetic position'.

He continued on well-trodden ground from there, arguing that the 'poetic school' frequently loses sight of the protagonist's psychology in place of the externalities and minutiae of everyday life. He wrote that such films get bogged down by 'abstract symbolism', and lack a contemporary theme, preferring instead to reveal exotic locations and ethnographic details. In the middle of the article, he argued:

> 'The school' [as he facetiously calls 'poetic cinema' throughout the article] returns cinema to the origins of its natural spectacle. Therein lies its well-known innovation. It not only insists on using the methods of painting in the cinema, it also asserts a new essence of painting [*zhivopisnost'*].
>
> (Bleiman 1973: 527)

The problem with this idea – which Bleiman took directly from 'Eternal Motion' – was that cinema is not bound by the same limitations as painting; the limitations, he claimed, that define its 'essence'. Thus, Paradjanov's claim to reinvent cinema through painting lacked an organic basis in the form itself. At the same time, '"the school" rejects literary representation' (Bleiman 1973: 528) and its 'poetics are oriented only toward legends and parables' (1973: 535) that are locked into a closed system of allusions [*inoskazaniia*], the comprehension of which deliberately evades the spectator's reasonable abilities. The power of Bleiman's analysis of *Shadows* and its influence on cinema during the late 1960s was that it possessed a strong component of the truth. But the author ended on a sinister note when he argued that the problem with 'the school' is not a question of style; the problem is at the root of its aesthetic principles, and its 'inner contradictions lead [the school] to a permanent crisis' (1973: 541). In other words, even the best that poetic cinema had to offer, e.g. *Shadows*, is ultimately a failure. Consequently, he implied, Soviet cinema must reject 'the school', and especially its most talented and accomplished master, Sergei Paradjanov.

Bleiman claimed that his article was 'not a judgement, but a conversation [*ne prigovor, a razgovor*]', yet the first response to his article in *Iskusstvo kino* – from Ivan Dziuba no less – was rejected for publication, in part because of the latter author's spotty political record, and in part because of its forceful tone toward a venerable senior colleague. As in his earlier work, *Internationalism or Russification?*, Dziuba (1989: 60-82) knew how to argue using Central Committee talking points, writing that *Shadows*' 'ethnographic and folkloric motifs' were 'strictly subordinated to the task of understanding the life of the people and revealing the fate of the heroes'. He furthermore iterated that *Shadows* was categorically 'opposed to the exotic film, and films in which the ethnographic and folkloric elements [...] simply play a decorative or sensationalistic role' (1989: 65). Instead, he interpreted the film's treatment of folklore and ethnography as emerging from the social conditions of the people of the Carpathians and, by extension, of Ukraine. Finally, Dziuba underlined that this is an authorial driven project. *Shadows* was not just a document of Hutsul life, but 'Paradjanov's [own] understanding of the people's everyday life as a ritualized and aesthetic crystallization of [their] history' (1989: 66). Thus, the film is not only a celebration of the vibrant culture of the Hutsuls, but also an original cinematic expression. While such themes were common in several other reviews and retrospectives on *Shadows of Forgotten Ancestors*, Dziuba's history as an activist, and with the film itself during the premiere, transformed his innocuous defence of it into a thinly-veiled expression of Ukrainian 'bourgeois nationalism'.

In the September 1971 issue, however, *Iskusstvo kino* allowed the prolific literary scholar Lev Anninskii to respond to Bleiman, although he wisely left the author's name and article out. While admitting the difficulty of *Shadows* for the audience, he proposed to try to reveal 'the ethical secret of the picture', suggesting in the process, pace Dziuba, that such difficulty did not condemn it as entirely closed off from an outside understanding. Anninskii argued that, far from being an ethnographic collection of exotic objects, dances and songs whose arbitrary symbolic code can only be broken by its own creators, Paradjanov made a film that offers a sustained glimpse into the 'existence of the Hutsul [...] from the inside – a psychological' image (Anninskii 1971: 140–41). Thus, the critic finds in the film exactly what its detractors claimed was absent, namely a psychological basis to the hero's actions. Here, however, Anninskii also denied that the importance of *Shadows* exists in its ability to represent the particular space of Bukovina and, by extension, a type of Ukrainian national essence. Instead, the animistic culture of the Hutsuls on display is merely the surface under which lies a deeply ethical basis in defence of the world of the individual (1971: 146). Like Bleiman, Anninskii used *Shadows of Forgotten Ancestors* to speak to the broader movement of 'poetic cinema', a topic that critics in Moscow continued to debate for a few more years. Nevertheless, Anninskii's article would be the last sustained analysis of Paradjanov's film in the Soviet Union until the late 1980s, when both Dziuba's and Solov'eva and Shitova's articles finally reached the public.

Bleiman continued to have a direct relationship to the director's fate. A year after 'Archaicists or Innovators'? was published, Paradjanov returned to Kiev to adapt another Kotsiubyns'kyi novel for the screen (the autobiographical *Intermezzo*, published in 1908). Significantly, Goskino placed Bleiman in charge of the internal review of the screenplay, where he reiterated his earlier analysis of the director's visual and narrative style, but put the question more directly:

> We need to decide principally and decisively, can our cinema be so generous as to make pictures in such an individual style as Paradjanov's style? If not, then it is necessary to say directly [...] that Paradjanov will not find a place in [...] our cinema.
>
> (RGALI 2944/4/2145a: 5)

He concluded the internal review in even starker language: 'The question is this: Will Paradjanov work or not work?' (RGALI 2944/4/2145a: 7). Bleiman pleaded ignorance in answer to his own question and asked the Central Committee of the Communist Party to resolve it.

The answer came the following Monday, when the head of the CPU Cultural Affairs Department, Fedchenko, reported on an iconostasis that Paradjanov had taken from the village of Kosmach in the Carpathians for use in the first church scene in *Shadows*. Although Paradjanov was obliged to return the icons after five months, the report stated that he had refused to do so, and the antiquities were still in his possession until recently, or had been given to the State Museum of Ukrainian Decorative Arts 'without the consent of the residents of Kosmach' (TsDAHOU 1/25/515: 60). Although all the pieces were recovered, the report ends with a call to prosecute those individuals responsible for such a 'gross violation of socialist legality' (TsDAHOU 1/25/515: 61). The following month, Fedchenko commented more directly on Bleiman's question in a report to the Central Committee that stated Paradjanov's screenplay 'is written in a style alien to the method of Socialist Realism' (TsDAHOU 1/25/515: 32). It furthermore blamed Sviatoslav Ivanov for taking 'Paradjanov under his personal guardianship' (TsDAHOU 1/25/515: 33). Apparently, Shelest too had decided to prevent the director from working in Ukraine. Ivanov wrote to the beleaguered First Secretary in January to remind him of *Shadows*, which brought Ukrainian cinema 'to the international screen after a prolonged interruption' (Briukhovets'ka 2001: 175–76). After this letter, Shelest gave the director a lifeline until he too lost his job in Ukraine. Paradjanov left for Moscow and returned to Ukraine once more in December 1973, only to be arrested. As he sat in jail in late 1975, he wrote to his sister Ruzanna to brag about Mikhail Bleiman's fateful article, 'Archaicists or Innovators?' Paradjanov claimed: 'This article is about me. It talks about the "school" that I created. I created it, they destroyed it, and that's it. That's the meaning of my isolation' (Zakoian 2000: 97).

By this time, however, Paradjanov had already denounced *Shadows*, saying during a speech in December 1971: 'I have absolutely stepped aside from that ethnographic film, which was so colonial, and I believe that it is a sign of a colossal disease in a young man if such a master as Iurii Illienko imitates it' (Paradzhanov 2001–02: 11–33). Nonetheless, this is the film that would remain his legacy. Andrei Tarkovsky and Viktor Shklovskii wrote to Shcherbyts'kyi in April 1974 pleading for Paradjanov's release: '*Shadows of Forgotten Ancestors* proved not only to Ukraine, but to all Ukrainians scattered about the world by centuries of turmoil, that only in the Soviet Union has the voice of Ukrainian art spoken fully and clearly' (Tarkovsky 1991: 94). Another letter addressed to Brezhnev and Shcherbyts'kyi, and signed by such names as Burt Lancaster, Robert De Niro and Philip Roth, mentioned him only as the director of *Shadows of Forgotten Ancestors* (Steffen 2013: 94–97). By this time, references to the director and his most important film were excised from print in the Soviet Union. One indication of the degree to which Paradjanov's film had been excised from Soviet film history in the mid-1970s was Valerii Fomin's thorough analysis of poetic cinema in 'Mezhdu poeziei i prozoi'/'Between Poetry and Prose' (1975). While examining the body of work that Bleiman identified as 'the school' in a rigorous and sophisticated manner, Fomin (1975) omitted any mention of Paradjanov or *Shadows*, preferring (or compelled) instead to focus on the Georgian film-makers Tengiz Abuladze and Giorgi Shengelia, along with Tarkovsky.

Chapter 5
Conclusion: Fifty years later

Shadows of Forgotten Ancestors returned to the Soviet public sphere during perestroika, after Paradjanov made his final two films in the Caucasus – *Ambavi Suramis tsikhisa/The Legend of Suram Fortress* (1985) and *Ashiki Keribi/Ashik-Kerib* (1989). By the late 1990s, several books had been published in Russia, Ukraine, Armenia and Georgia on Paradjanov, although of course not only about *Shadows*. Illienko, Luhovs'kyi and other members of the cast and crew published their memoirs about the making of *Shadows*, in many ways reaffirming its legendary status within the Soviet canon, and as an essential moment in the movement toward a Ukrainian national consciousness. The Ukrainian magazines *Kino-kolo/Cinema Circle* and *Kino Teatr/Cinema and Theatre* dedicated several articles and even whole issues to *Shadows* and Paradjanov's time in Ukraine. Soviet-era debates about the film – whether its essence lies in its ethnographic beauty, or in its psychological and moral depth – seem hopelessly dated, and most post-Soviet critics seem entirely unconcerned with the essential 'problems' that Bleiman identified with 'the school'. In fact, Paradjanov's interest in beautiful old things now supports the widespread agreement about his eccentric 'genius', an idea that film-makers Serge Avedikian and Olena Fetisova reproduce ad nauseum in their French-Ukrainian biopic, *Paradjanov* (2013).

Yet the commemoration of the film could take on an extremely localized meaning too. The Paliichuk home is preserved in the village of Verkhovyna in south-western Ukraine as a *Shadows of Forgotten Ancestors*

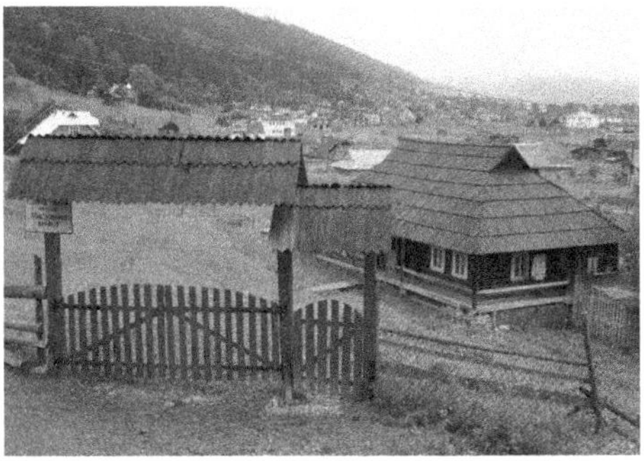

Figure 25: Entrance to the *Shadows of Forgotten Ancestors* Museum, Verkhovyna, Ukraine. Photograph by EugeneB.

Architectural Museum. In this local Carpathian context, however, Paradjanov becomes irrelevant to the film, and actor (and later screenwriter and director) Ivan Mykolaichuk emerges as its important auteur. Upon his tragic death at the age of 46 in 1987, the Carpathian-born actor was even acknowledged as the film's real genius by none other than Paradjanov himself, in what appeared as a rare moment of humility (Paradzhanov 1987). In his 2004 history of Ukrainian cinema, Dovzhenko Studios film-maker Vasyl' Illiashenko (2004: 267) called Mykolaichuk 'the symbol of Ukraine and its essence [...]. There are a lot of talented actors. There are enough of them in any [national] cinema. But actor-messiahs are a rarity. It happened that *Shadows* presented Ukraine [with] the rebellious soul of Ivan'.

During the 50th anniversary of the 4 September premiere in 2015, Paradjanov, Mykolaichuk and Illienko (all now deceased) were all properly acknowledged, but organizers of the event also made efforts to acknowledge the importance of Russian actress Larisa Kadochnikova in her role as Marichka, along with the courage of Ivan Dziuba and other dissidents who protested politically-motivated arrests in 1965. *Shadows of Forgotten Ancestors* has become a centrepiece of the Ukrainian 1960s. After an initial flurry of interest in Paradjanov in Russia during the 1990s, however, interest has tapered off. *Iskusstvo kino* published only three substantive articles on the director in the last fifteen years in comparison to the countless articles on every facet of the life and work of Andrei Tarkovsky. Perhaps because Russians have a much more 'Russian' auteur in Tarkovsky to build the myth of a cinematic genius, Paradjanov is less necessary there. More interesting and important in the present day, however, is the currency that *Shadows* has acquired in the growing field of Central or East European cinema, and in its influence on other film-makers such as Abbas Kiarostami. That, however, is a story for a different book.

References

ARCHIVAL SOURCES

Archival references are given in the text as follows: Fond number, inventory number [*opis'*] / document number [*edinitsa khraneniia*] sheet number.

Russian State Archive of Literature and Art [Rossiiskii gosudarstvennyi arkhiv literatury i iskusstva, RGALI]
Fond 2936: Union of Film-makers of the USSR.
Opis' 1: Documents of the Secretariat.
Opis' 4: Documents from Union Plenums and Congresses.
Fond 2944: State Committee for Cinematography (Goskino).
Opis' 4: Documents from the Production Department.

Central State Archive-Museum of Literature and Art of Ukraine [Tsentral'nyi derzhavnyi arkhiv-muzei literatury i mystetstva Ukrainy, TsDAMLMU]
Fond 655: Union of Film-makers of the Ukrainian SSR.
Opis 1: General Documents.
Fond 670: Aleksandr Dovzhenko Feature Film Studio, Kiev.
Opis' 1: Administrative Documents.
Opis' 2: Screenplays.
Fond 1127: State Committee on Cinematography, Ukrainian SSR (Derzhkino), Screenplay-Editorial Board.
Opis' 1: General Documents.

Central State Archive of the Federal Government of Ukraine [Tsentral'nyi derzhavnyi arkhiv vyshyi orhaniv vlasti Ukrainy, TsDAVOU]
Fond 4754: State Committee on Cinematography, Ukrainian SSR (Derzhkino).
Opis' 1: General Documents.

Central State Archive of Social Organizations of Ukraine [Tsentral'nyi derzhavnyi arkhiv hromads'kykh orhanizatsii Ukrainy, TsDAHOU]
Fond 1: Central Committee of the Communist Party of Ukraine.
Opis' 1: Documents of the First Secretary.

PUBLISHED SOURCES

Adrianova, Nadiia (1965), 'Problemy dubliuvannia', *Kul'tura i zhyttia*, 1 April, p. 4.

Anninskii, Lev (1971), 'Tri zvena', *Iskusstvo kino*, 9, pp. 134–52.

Anon (1965), 'Do novykh uspikhiv, dorohi Dovzhenkivtsi!', *Kul'tura i zhyttia*, 8 April, p. 4.

Anon (1966a), 'Rishennia zhiuri po khudozhnikh fil'makh', *Kul'tura i zhyttia*, 2 June, p. 4.

Anon (1966b), '"Tini zabutykh predkiv" na mizhnarodnomu kinofestyvali', *Kul'tura i zhyttia*, 25 September, p. 3.

Babyshkin, Oleh (1966), *Ukrains'ka literatura na ekrani: literaturno-krytychnyi narys*, Kyiv: Radians'kyi pysmennyk.

Baskakov, Vladimir (1996), 'Kak zamorozili kinematograf "ottepeli"...', in Valerii Fomin (ed.), *Kino i vlast': Sovetskoe kino, 1965–1985*, Moscow: Materik, pp. 132–43.

Bleiman, Mikhail (1970), 'Arkhaisty ili novatory?', *Iskusstvo kino*, 7, pp. 55–76. Reprinted in Bleiman (1973), pp. 506–541.

----- (1973), *O kino – svidetel'skie pokazaniia*, Moscow: Iskusstvo.

Blokhin, Nikolai (2002), *Izgnanie Paradzhanova*, Stavropol'.

Brainchenko, F. (2001), 'Dopovidna zapyska dyrektora kinoteatru "Ukraina" pislia prem"iery fil'mu "Tini zabutykh predkiv"', in Larysa Briukhovets'ka (ed.), *Poetychne kino: zaboronena shkola*, Kyiv: ArtEk/Kino-teatr, pp. 268–69.

Briukhovets'ka, Larysa (1999), 'Heorhii Iakutovych i poetychne kino', *Kino teatr*, 6, pp. 2–4.

----- (ed.) (2001), *Poetychne kino: zaboronena shkola*, Kiev: ArtEk/Kino-teatr.

----- (2004), 'Kino iak svitohliad: Dovzhenko i Paradzhanov', *Kino teatr*, 3, http://www.ktm.ukma.kiev.ua/show_content.php?id=319. Accessed 24 March 2005.

Briukhovets'ka, Ol'ha (2002), 'Do pytannia "poetychnoho kino"', *Kino teatr*, 4, pp. 26–30.

----- (2012), 'Ukrains'ke poetychne kino v konteksti natsional'noho pytannia SRSR', *Teoriia ta istoriia kul'tura*, Naukovi zapysky NaUKMA 127, Kyiv: NaUKMA Press, pp. 40–45.

Chufus, Bohdan (1967), 'Lyst do kinomyttsiv', *Novyny kinoekrana*, 6, p. 4.

Crowther, Bosley (1966), 'Film festival: "The Hunt"', *The New York Times*, 20 September, p. 39.

Dolidze, Siko (1964), 'Lyst z Gruzii: Radiiemo razom z vamy', *Radians'ka ku'tura*, 19 November, p. 4.

Drach, Ivan (1965), 'Spasibo!', *Literaturnaia Rossiia*, 26 February, p. 17.

Dziuba, Ivan (1989), 'Otkrytie ili zakrytie "shkoly"?', *Iskusstvo kino*, 11, pp. 60–82.

Efird, Robert (2014), 'Amorphous forms: Time and subjectivity in *Shadows of Forgotten Ancestors*', *Studies in Russian and Soviet Cinema*, 8: 1, pp. 24–40.

First, Joshua (2014), *Ukrainian Cinema: Belonging and Identity during the Soviet Thaw*, London: I.B. Tauris.

Fomin, Valerii (1975), 'Mezhdu poeziei i prozoi', in Valerii Fomin (ed.), *Kinopanorama: Sovetskoe kino segodnia*, Moscow: Iskusstvo, pp. 111–48.

Gazda, Ianush (1966), 'Hutsul'ska balada', in Larysa Briukhovets'ka (ed.) (2001), *Poetychne kino: zaboronena shkola*, Kyiv: ArtEk/Kino-Teatr, pp. 31–32.

Grigorian, Levon (2011), *Paradzhanov*, Moscow: Molodaia gvardiia.

Gulyan, Yuliya (2013), 'Filmic collage: Poetics of myth in Sergei Parajanov's oeuvres', MA thesis, Amsterdam: University of Amsterdam.

Gurga, J. J. (2012), 'Echoes of the past: Ukrainian poetic cinema and the experiential ethnographic mode', Ph.D. thesis, London: University College London.

Hoseiko, Liubomyr (2005), *Istoriia ukrains'koho kinematohrafa, 1896–1995*, Kyiv: Kino-kolo. First published 2001.

Illienko, Iurii (1972), 'Voobrazhaemoe interv'iu', *Iskusstvo kino*, 11, pp. 126–36.

----- (2008a), *IurkA illienkA dopovidna Apostolovi PeTRu: avtoportret al'ter ego (Sebe inshoho) vnaturIE: roman-kharaman: Kniga 1*, Ternopil': Bohdan.

----- (2008b), *IurkA illienkA dopovidna Apostolovi PeTRu: avtoportret al'ter ego (Sebe inshoho) vnaturIE: roman-kharaman: Kniga 3*, Ternopil': Bohdan.

Illiashenko, Vasyl' (2004), *Istoriia ukrains'koho kinomystetstva*, Kyiv: Vik.

Ivanov, Sviatoslav (1973), 'Ukrains'kyi khudozhnii fil'm 60-kh rokiv', in Larysa Briukhovets'ka (ed.) (2001), *Poetychne kino: zaboronena shkola*, Kyiv: ArtEk/Kino-Teatr, pp. 229–43.

Jakobsen, Kiesten (2014), 'Modalities of the long take in the era of late socialism: Miklos Jansco, Sergei Parajanov, Andrei Tarkovsky', Ph.D. thesis, Stanford, CA: Stanford University.

Kondratenko, Oleksandr (1964), 'Poeziia hlybokoho dramatyzmu', *Radians'ka kul'tura*, 20 September, p. 2.

Korniienko, Ivan (ed.) (1968), *Fil'm i doba*, Kyiv: Mystetstvo.

Korobchak, L. (1964), 'Podviinyi debiut', *Radians'ka kul'tura*, 3 December, p. 4.

Korol', Renata (2001), 'Tak pochynavsia vydatnyi fil'm', in Larysa Briukhovets'ka (ed.), *Poetychne kino: zaboronena shkola*, Kyiv: ArtEk/Kino-Teatr, pp. 319–20.

Kotsiubyns'kyi, Mykhailo (1967), *Tini zabutykh predkiv*, Kyiv: Dnipro.

Koval', V. (1993), 'Iak neznyshchennyi sobor', *Molod' Ukrainy*, 2 April.

Krawchenko, Bohdan (1985), *Social Change and National Consciousness in Twentieth-Century Ukraine*, London: Macmillan Press.

Kudriavtsev, Sergei (2006), 'Otechestvennye fil'my v sovetskom kinoprokate', 7 April, http://kinanet.livejournal.com/14172.html#cutid1. Accessed 3 January 2016.

Kyryliuk, Evhen (1965), 'Pravda, opovyta romantykoiu', *Literaturna Ukraina*, 17 September, p. 3.

Lakatosh, Robert (1999), 'Traditsiia i novatorstvo v strukturuvanni zobrazhennia u fil'makh Serhiia Paradzhanova', *Kino teatr*, 5, pp. 2–4.

Lewytzkyj, Borys (1984), *Politics and Society in Soviet Ukraine, 1953–1980*, Edmonton: Canadian Institute of Ukrainian Studies of Alberta.

Luhovs'kyi, Volodymyr (1998), Tini zabutykh predkiv *rozkadrovky: Nevidomyi maestro*, Kyiv: Kino-Teatr.

Martin, Terry (2001), *The Affirmative Action Empire: Nations and Nationalism in the Soviet Union, 1923–1939*, Ithaca, NY: Cornell University Press.

Musiienko, Dmytro (1964), 'Khvala zhyttiu', *Novyny kinoekrana*, 12, pp. 4–5.

Mykolaichuk, Ivan (1991), 'Daleka podorozh', in Mariia Ievhen'evna Mykolaichuk (ed.), *Bilyi ptakh z chornoiu oznakoiu: Ivan Mykolaichuk: spohady, interv'iu, stsenarii*, Kyiv: Mystetstvo, pp. 212–19.

Nebesio, Bohdan (1994), '*Shadows of Forgotten Ancestors*: Storytelling in the novel and the film', *Literature/Film Quarterly*, 22: 1, pp. 42–49.

Paradzhanov, Sergei (1966), 'Vechnoe dvizhenie', *Iskusstvo kino*, 1, pp. 60–66.

----- (1987), 'Nezvazhaiuchy na vidstani', *Literaturna Ukraina*, 20 August, p. 6.

----- (1990), '"...chtoby ne molchat', berus' za pero": Vybrannye mesta iz perepiski s nedrugami i druz'iami', *Iskusstvo kino*, 12, pp. 32–34.

----- (2001–02), 'Sergei Paradjanov's speech in Minsk before the creative and scientific youth of Byelorussia on 1 December 1971' (trans. Nora Seligman Favorov and P. Elana Pick), *Armenian Review*, 47/48: 3–4 and 1–2, pp. 11–33.

Pasolini, Pier Paolo (2001), 'The "Cinema of Poetry"', in John Orr and Olga Taxidou (eds), *Post-War Cinema and Modernity: A Film Reader*, New York: New York University Press, pp. 37–53.

Payne, Robert (1990), 'The storm of the eye: Culture, spectacle, Paradzhanov', *Spectator*, 10: 1, pp. 32–45.

Petrovskii, Miron (1965), 'Gutsul'skaia poema', *Uchitel'skaia gazeta*, 7 January, p. 4.

Poltarats'kyi, Oleksii (1968), 'O nekrytychne isliduvannia', *Mystetstvo*, 2, p. 35.

Rubchak, Bohdan (1981), 'The music of Satan and the bedeviled world: An essay on Mykhailo Kotsiubynsky', in Mikhailo Kotsiubynsky (ed.), *Shadows of Forgotten Ancestors*, Littleton, CO: Canadian Institute of Ukrainian Studies by Ukrainian Academic Press, pp. 79–121.

Shelest, Petro (1970), *Ukraino, nasha Radians'ka*, Kyiv: Politychna literatura.

Shevchuk, Yuri (2005), 'The bold vision of Kira Muratova and its distorted reflection in New York', *The Ukrainian Weekly*, 27 February, http://www.ukrweekly.com/old/archive/2005/090529.shtml. Accessed 12 January 2016.

Shlapak, Dmytro (1965), '*Tini zabutykh predkiv*', *Na ekranakh Kyieva*, 16 October, p. 1.

----- (1966), 'Ospivuvaty velych narodu', *Novyny kinoekrana*, 3, p. 1.

Shnitseri, Liuda and Zhan [Jean] (1966), 'Zarubizhna presa pro ukrains'ki fil'my', *Novyny kinoekrana*, 9, p. 6.

Solov'eva, Inna and Shitova, Vera (1989), 'Nakoplenie ustoichivosti', *Iskusstvo kino*, 11, pp. 83–91.

Stankevych, Kateryna (1964), 'Stsenarii chy skhemarii?', *Molod' Ukrainy*, 1 November, p. 3.

Steffen, James (2013), *The Cinema of Sergei Parajanov*, Madison, WI: University of Wisconsin Press.

Tarkovsky, Andrei (1991), *Time within Time: The Diaries, 1970–1986*, London and New York: Verso.

Taylor, Richard (2001), *The Battleship Potemkin* (The KINO Film Companion 1), London: I.B. Tauris.

Tereshchenko, Oles' (2015), 'Spetsvypusk. 50-richchia prem"iery strichky "Tini zabutykh predkiv"', *Pro holovne*, 4 September, https://youtu.be/pbFoE1n5-b4. Accessed 28 October 2015.

Thompson, Kristin (1986), 'The concept of cinematic excess', in Philip Rosen (ed.), *Narrative, Apparatus, Ideology: A Film Theory Reader*, New York: Columbia University Press, pp. 130–34.

Thompson, Kristin and Bordwell, David (2003), *Film History: An Introduction*, 2nd ed., Boston, MA: McGraw Hill.

Trofimenkov, Mikhail (1999), '"Novaia volna" – sorok let spustia', *Iskusstvo kino*, 5, http://kinoart.ru/archive/1999/05/n5-article24. Accessed 7 January 2016.

Turbin, Vladimir (1964), 'Mir, otkrytyi zanovo', *Komsomol'skaia Pravda*, 27 December, p. 4.

----- (1965), 'Zhivoi ogon'', *Molodaia gvardiia*, 2, pp. 280–91.

Vergelis, Oleg (2002), 'Sladkogolosaia ptitsa iz kletki', *Russkii zhurnal*, 6 September, http://www.russ.ru/culture/cinema/20020906_ver.html. Accessed 13 March 2005.

Vlasov, Marat (1997), 'Kinoiskusstvo i epokha zastoia', in Marat Vlasov (ed.), *Sovetskoe kino semidesiatykh – pervoi poloviny vos'midesiatykh godov: uchebnoe posobie*, Moscow: VGIK, pp. 3–14.

Yekelchyk, Serhy (2007), *Ukraine: Birth of a Modern Nation*, Oxford: Oxford University Press.

Youngblood, Denise J. (2014), *Bondarchuk's War and Peace: Literary Classic to Soviet Cinematic Epic*, Lawrence, KS: University of Kansas Press.

Zakoian, Garegin (ed.) (2000), *Sergei Paradzhanov: Pis'ma iz zony*, Yerevan: Fil'madaran.

Zinych, Volodymyr (1964), 'Interes do etnohrafii', review of Olena Kravets, *M.M. Kotsiubyns'kyi pro narodnyi pobut*, *Literaturna Ukraina*, 15 September, p. 3.

Zorin, Ia. (1965), 'Liubov"iu dorozhyt' umiite...', *Kul'tura i zhyttia*, 9 September, p. 4.

Notes

1. https://commons.wikimedia.org/wiki/File:Verhovyna_Paradzhanov_museum.jpg.
2. *Shadows* was not exactly a 'flop' either, as many other famous Soviet films performed much worse. For example, Andrei Tarkovsky's celebrated film *Andrei Rublev* (1966) sold less than three million tickets. According to Marat Vlasov (1997: 9), the average film during the Brezhnev era only garnered eleven million viewers. Thus, the few blockbusters like Leonid Gaidai's *'Operatsiia Y' i drugie prikliucheniia Shurika/'Operation Y' and Shurik's Further Adventures* (1965, 70 million viewers) and Vladimir Basov's *Shchit i mech/The Shield and Sword* (1968, 68 million viewers) subsidized the mass of undifferentiated socialist realist works, and the few art films from renowned directors like Paradjanov and Tarkovsky (Kudriavtsev 2006).
3. Illienko first related this story himself to several people, including Paradjanov's biographer, Levon Grigorian (2011: 105). The legend is reproduced in the French-Ukrainian biopic about the film-maker, *Paradjanov* (Avedikian, 2013).
4. In the interwar era (1919–39), the historic province of Galicia belonged to Poland and Bukovina to Romania. As part of the Molotov-Ribbentrop Pact of 1939, the Soviet Union was awarded these 'Ukrainian' territories, and they were attached to the Ukrainian SSR that year. From the outbreak of war with Nazi Germany in 1941 until 1944, the Germans controlled these regions, but they were reincorporated into Ukraine during the latter year, where they remain to the present day.
5. Paradjanov's demand for a million roubles probably had something to do with the incredibly large budget that Sergei Bondarchuk's adaptation of *Voina i mir/War and Peace* (1966) had been awarded around the same time (Youngblood 2014: 15). Paradjanov would later associate Bondarchuk's film with everything that was wrong with Soviet cinema at the beginning of the 1970s (Paradzhanov 2001–2002: 18).
6. Initially, the studio awarded Paradjanov with a 1000 rouble honorarium (a third of the total sum), along with a secondary screenwriting credit. Eventually, the director demanded half the honorarium and that his name would appear above that of Chendei in the credits, much to the latter's chagrin (TsDAMLMU 670/1/1581: 58–59; Luhovs'kyi 1998: 41).
7. Illienko admitted that he 'lost' the war with Paradjanov, but, in the process, the 'film won' (Illienko 2008a: 5–6).
8. Both actors would struggle with acceptance at the studio, even though they made a significant effort to learn Ukrainian for their roles. Kadochnikova would remain in Ukraine as Illienko's wife and acted in many of his films. After their divorce in 1975, however, she reported that the entire film community in Kiev shunned her, largely, she claims, because she was Russian (Vergelis 2002). Nonetheless, Oles' Tereshchenko (2015) interviewed Kadochnikova on Ukraine's Pershyi Kanal (Channel 1) for the 2015 gala 50th anniversary of the *Shadows of Forgotten Ancestors* premiere, perhaps indicating a renewed appreciation of her role in the film.
9. Paradjanov was still insistent on the Muscovite until the studio leadership and other members of the cast and crew supported the young actor (Luhovs'kyi 1998: 41–49).
10. The term 'Little Russians' to refer to Ukrainians emerged in the Russian Empire during the nineteenth century. It functioned to deny a distinct Ukrainian nationality, while identifying the colourful but primitive dialect and folkways of the peasants west of the Don River (Yekelchyk 2007: 38).

11. In this 1972 interview, Illienko also acknowledged influence from the entire Soviet canon of great cinematographers, such as Iurii Ekel'chik, Daniil Demutskii, Anatolii Golovnia, along with his VGIK professor Boris Volchek, all of whom were stylistically within the classical tradition of high Stalinism. Thus, Illienko's sole statement about his influences while making *Shadows* is fraught with a heavy dose of political correctness.
12. Paradjanov (1966: 62–63) heavily criticized *Oleksa Dovbush* in 'Eternal Motion', calling it a false and inauthentic representation of Hutsul life and the Carpathian landscape.
13. *Kresani* are black hats worn by Hutsuls and other Carpathian highlanders that resemble bowlers, but are often adorned with bands of embroidery around the crown.
14. *Kozy* can also refer to children.
15. We might understand this image as part of the ethnic colour of the Carpathians, as this is one of the few areas of Ukraine that traditionally engaged in corn production prior to the 1950s.
16. In Kotsiubyns'kyi's text, Vasyl' is also victim to the Paliichuk-Hutentiuk feud (Kotsiubyns'kyi 1967: 13).
17. *Brynza* is related to feta cheese in its soft, flaky texture. It is made from sheep's milk.
18. A *bokorash* is a type of log driver common to Hutsulshchyna, who bring timber down the Cheremosh River to the saw mills in villages. One of Heorhii Yakutovych's most famous paintings before working on *Shadows* was a study of a group of *bokorashi* (Briukhovets'ka 1999: 2).
19. Dziuba (1989: 81) argues that the biblical metaphor of the lamb is less relevant to *Shadows* than the social explanation for their importance. Then again, he was writing in the Soviet Union and trying to defend the film against its naysayers in the Central Committee and Goskino.
20. The sorcerer was played by Georgian actor Spartak Bagashvili, a Stalin Prize winner, of whom Paradjanov was constantly terrified. Instead of speaking to Bagashvili directly, he asked his assistant director, Volodymyr Luhovs'kyi, to give him his directions on the set (Luhovs'kyi 1996: 49–51).
21. Tarkovsky was also enamoured with Bruegel, and the painter's 'The Hunters in the Snow' (1565) prominently appears in *Soliaris/Solaris* (1972).
22. According to Terry Martin (2001: 432), the 'Friendship of the Peoples was the officially sanctioned metaphor of an imagined multinational community' in the Soviet Union after 1935.

www.ingramcontent.com/pod-product-compliance
Lightning Source LLC
LaVergne TN
LVHW080831240826
846232LV00015B/57
9781783207091